D0954182

RUNNING IN CIRCLES

How False Spirituality Traps Us in Unhealthy Relationships

Kim V. Engelmann

FOREWORD BY John Ortberg

IVP Books

An imprint of InterVarsity Press
Downers Grove, Illinois

InterVarsity Press
P.O. Box 1400, Downers Grove, IL 60515-1426
World Wide Web: www.ivpress.com
E-mail: email@ivpress.com

InterVarsity Press® is the book-publishing division of InterVarsity Christian Fellowship/USA®, a student
movement active on campus at hundreds of universities, colleges and schools of nursing in the United States of
America, and a member movement of the International Fellowship of Evangelical Students. For information
about local and regional activities, write Public Relations Dept., InterVarsity Christian Fellowship/USA, 6400
Schroeder Rd., P.O. Box 7895, Madison, WI 53707-7895, or visit the IVCF website at <www.intervarsity.org>.

Design: Cindy Kiple
Images: Images.com/Corbis

ISBN 978-0-8308-3317-7

Printed in the United States of America ∞

Library of Congress Cataloging-in-Publication Data

Engelmann, Kim.
   Running in circles: how false spirituality traps us in unhealthy
   relationships/Kim V. Engelmann.
      p. cm.
   Includes bibliographical references and index.
   ISBN 978-0-8308-3317-7 (pbk.: alk. paper)
   1. Interpersonal relations—Religious aspects—Christianity. 2.
   Conflict management—Religious aspects—Christianity. 3. Religious
   addiction. 4. Compulsive behavior—Religious aspects—Christianity.
   I. Title.
   BV4597.52.E54 2007
   248.4—dc22
                                                      2007011612

P	18	17	16	15	14	13	12	11	10	9	8	7	6	5	4	3	2	1
Y	22	21	20	19	18	17	16	15	14	13	12	11	10	09	08	07		

Contents

Foreword

There is a strange paradox deep in the soul. Years ago, I was part of a survey that asked thousands of people what had most helped them grow spiritually. The number one answer was pain. Times of suffering and difficulty had a way of making people aware of their frailty and lack of control. The painful stages remind us how, in times of "normalcy," we can focus so easily on money or prestige or things that do not really amount to much. They shatter our self-sufficiency. They open us up to receiving the truth about ourselves. When biblical writers like James say that suffering has the power to bring about maturity in the human soul, they are simply making observations about the way things are.

Here's the other side of the paradox. Ask ten people what the number-one reason is why they doubt the existence of God. Nine of them will say it is the existence of pain and suffering in the world. We cannot fathom why there is so much hurt, so deep and so unexplained. We cannot understand why a good, loving and competent God does not come down and fix up this mess. Now. Today. We see bad things happen to good people and have no easy formula to reassure them. Or ourselves. When biblical writers like Job cry out against unexplained suffering in the world, they cry out for us.

It is this tension that lies at the heart of Kim's book. There is a kind of suffering that can produce growth and good in the human soul. Suffering is never a good thing in and of itself. But it can produce good fruit. On the other hand, there is a destructive kind of suffering, which we are called not to endure but to end, to flee, to protest.

Knowing the difference takes discernment. It's a little like physical training. I had a friend who was in great shape and wanted me to move a little more in that direction. He would tell me it involved a certain level of discomfort. It's the tearing of tissue (also known as lifting weights) that causes them to be rebuilt stronger than ever. However, if you do not have a wise and discerning friend to help you, you may tear too much or tear the wrong thing.

Kim Engelmann can be that wise and discerning friend. She is uniquely qualified. She has endured soul-wrenching pain in her own life, and you'll see some of that story in these pages. She and her husband, Tim, have walked together through the deepest valleys of life. She is also a pastor and a shepherd who cannot help but listen and care for people in the rawest condition. With a tremendous mind and the pen of an artist, she can portray deep truths about God and the soul in ways that are compelling and unforgettable. For the past three-and-a-half years I have gotten to work alongside her and listen and learn from her, and now you do too.

So you have received a gift. Much of the secret of life is learning to get off the hamster wheel of fruitless suffering while remaining on the Potter's wheel. Kim will help you learn the difference. Read on.

John Ortberg

1

Trapped in a Cycle of Pain

And you call yourself a Christian!"

I noticed how tight and white my mother's lips were when she spoke. She was standing on the stair landing above me, hands on her hips.

"You'll never get into heaven with an attitude like that! God knows all the evil thoughts you've ever had about me. Not one is hidden from him."

She continued down the steps, her index finger pointed at me. Her footsteps were heavy, the stubby heels of her black shoes thudding. The thin pale lips were moving again.

"You'll never please God the way you are. Don't think you won't reap the consequences of your evil thoughts. 'Vengeance is mine. I will repay, says the Lord!'" She was upon me now.

I was eleven. I had vacuumed the house and, according to my mother, not done a very good job. I was not fond of vacuuming, and when she ordered me to do it over, I had pushed back. I thought I had done a great job, and besides, it was a daunting task. Our house was a historic faculty home on the campus of a well-endowed institution for higher learning. There were fireplaces in every room, and the rooms were immense.

Maybe she was angry because I had spent time with my father that morning listening to his lecture. He had read it to me with his glasses balanced on the end of his nose. She didn't like it when Dad and I spent time alone. But I wasn't really sure what had set off this episode. I never was.

"If you knew the truth—that I am the apple of God's eye—you would treat me differently!" She was building momentum now, her voice rising. "You are spurning God's chosen one when you look down on me!" The words shot through the air and whizzed through me with their familiar pain.

The culmination was at hand, the consequences imminent.

"You are a hypocrite—full of evil thoughts and lies. A whitewashed tomb. Everything you do and say is a lie, and Satan is the father of lies, so you must belong to him!"

I could hear the cicadas buzzing outside. There had been a rash of them that summer, and when you walked on the lawn you could scarcely avoid the sickening crunch they made underfoot. I was aware that I was crying.

"Go to your room!" she ordered, flinging her arm out to point up the stairs. "I don't want to see you again, and I don't want you to talk to anyone. Have nothing to do with your sister either. This family will not associate with someone who refuses to respect those God has put in authority over them!"

I ran up to my room and lay across the bed, sobbing. I cried like this almost every day. I sometimes wondered if other kids cried all the time, but I didn't have anyone to compare myself to. Outsiders weren't welcome in our home. When they did gain access, after a brief honeymoon the relationship was always cut off because of "questionable motives" or a "spiritual oppression" they brought with them.

Even my little sister's friend, a seven-year-old, was forbidden to come to our home to play. The tears and pleas of my sister, eight years younger than I, did not sway the decision. Friends were not easy to come by under these circumstances, and though I was only partially aware of it, I lived an isolated, lonely life. I was less favored than my sister, and I never had a real friend at all. I told myself I didn't need friends, that I was fine the way I was. I deadened myself to the circumstances, neutralizing any hopes and expectations. I said "Whatever" a lot.

Mine was a precarious life as well as a lonely one. I was constantly on edge, vigilant, able to emotionally prepare myself instantly for what could come my way at any second. You learn quickly when the only thing predictable is the unpredictable.

We'd be packed and ready to go on vacation, only to cancel on the day of departure because the trip was "not God's will." We'd be eagerly anticipating a promised outing or gift and it would be canceled or never delivered, again because of divine will. Pets were given away without discussion. We were dragged from church to church every couple of months, abandoning a congregation once the pastor said something that "disagreed with Scripture."

My father, a professor and theologian who was endlessly loyal to my mother, kept telling me it would get better, that God would do a new thing. He said this after each blowup, each tirade—and these could last for days.

I tried to believe him, and often after an eruption we experienced a period of calm. It was a scary calm—we weren't sure when things would flare up again—but it was a calm nonetheless, and I was grateful. Yet the pattern inevitably repeated itself, and despite our earnest prayers and hopes nothing changed. My father sometimes bore his soul to me. "Why does she have to be so cruel to you?" he would say after an angry outburst that had left me shattered and sullen.

I didn't know.

"She not only puts the knife in," he said, "but she turns it."

The fighting between my parents was extreme. Screaming and door slamming woke me in the night. Days of tension paralyzed my sister and me with fear, and we crept quietly up to the attic to play with old toys.

"I need to rise above this," Dad would tell me in his vulnerable moments after he had been the target of an onslaught. "I have to not let what she does affect me."

Away from home (and he kept the two worlds very separate) my father's work and writing helped a great many people come to know the authentic power of Jesus at work in their lives. His combination of intellectual knowledge and conviction of the personal presence of God flooded the lecture halls where he spoke. But the world at home was scary, insane and lonely.

As I grew older I discovered that my mother had been the victim of severe abuse as a child. Even though I intellectually began to come to terms with the reasons for her behavior, I was unable to free myself from her grasp. Still, my father's comments and judgments against my mother's behavior helped me begin to grasp the unfathomable and experience a deep courage. Despite her claim that she was God's voice and presence in the world, despite her grandiose proposals and assertions about her power and unique giftedness, I began to realize that she was—perhaps—wrong.

Maybe these experiences were not God's will at all. Perhaps it was wrong that I couldn't have friends over or get involved in social activities. Maybe I wasn't born to be miserable all the time, and maybe I wasn't in the grips of Satan with evil spirits lurking in dark corners ready to oppress me and throw me into hell. Maybe I wasn't contaminated by those demons the way my mother said I was when she came into my room in the middle of the night to cast them out. Perhaps purging the house of evil—praying in each room that Satan would leave—was not the way most families spent their Saturdays.

At one point I suggested to my father that we get Mom some help. His usually gentle face went rigid and he sucked in his breath. He told me my mother didn't need help, that she was doing better, and he asked where my family loyalty was. He declared that God had given him this situation so he could learn to rise above it. Jesus suffered, saints suffered—why shouldn't he?

This topic was clearly taboo. It was just too painful for my father to identify the problem honestly. So the bizarre, erratic behavior continued to loom larger than life and define us. One day her tirade might be God's voice to shape us up. Another day a low mood was a "dark night of the soul" she was being called to walk through. She often believed her struggles were demonic and had many well-known people in the deliverance ministry try to cast out spirits from her. It never seemed to take. Other days she accused my father of having no faith and contaminating her with an oppression she could not shake off.

Years of intensive psychotherapy later, as I look back at the shattered landscape of my early life, I still shudder at the cycle of pain and abuse. The most chilling aspect of those years was the fact that my mother's spiritual language seemed to validate everything. Although I am sure there were spiritual components to my mother's condition, her ultraspiritual terminology gave her assaults frightening leverage in our lives. If I had been able to grasp that my mother needed psychological help, perhaps I would not have taken her actions and words so much to heart. I would have had some mastery and control over the situation, and I would have had the correct words to define the reality in which I lived. Had my father been able to come to terms with the problem, I believe he would have attempted to persuade Mom to get professional help.

When I left for college, I watched from a distance as the situation became increasingly chaotic. During my visits home I saw my dad's jovial demeanor dissolve into brooding melancholy. He began to question why he was still alive. One day as he was walking out of a bank, he fell over with a massive stroke and died. He was only in his sixties.

Mom eventually left the area, and her behavior continued to deteriorate, especially once my father was gone. His presence had served as a kind of support for her erratic condition; once he died there was no one to contain it.

Our family's faith was a mixed blessing. Had we not believed in God, we might have sought help much more readily. Paradoxically, spiritual language can be a lacquer that covers over and justifies problems rather than helping us discern the most appropriate, even obvious, course of action.

I am a pastor now, and I see many people trapped in a similar cycle of pain. The woman in the abusive marriage whose husband threatens to kill her tells me, "Maybe if I just clean up that back room and keep the kitchen a little neater, things will get better. The Lord put me in this marriage, and God works all things for good." The wife of a bipolar man whose wild spending habits have brought them to financial ruin says, "God is telling me to love him and pray harder." There is certainly nothing wrong with loving, and praying harder is always warranted in difficult situations. But these people reappear in my office a week, a month, even a year or two later asking why God hasn't done anything. Despite their earnest prayers, heaven is silent. The old patterns keep repeating. There is no relief. In fact, the problem now looms larger than before.

I call this cycle "hamster-wheel suffering." In my work I have seen countless people who struggle with patterns of thought and behavior that keep them spinning but going nowhere. Unless we work through loss, trauma and abuse both psychologically and spiritually, we find ourselves muted, stymied and shut off from the present because of the past. The broad landscape of life grows dim and small. There seem to be no options. We cannot remember what used to bring us joy. Our sense of identity—if we ever had one—goes underground. Time collapses; we feel old or convince ourselves that life is almost over anyway. Dreams evaporate and fear interlaces even peaceful moments with dread. Delight, joy and wonder are replaced by obligation, guilt and routine.

When reading Dante's *Inferno* awhile back I was struck by how much of the torment in Dante's hell is cyclical. The people in one group are all stabbed in the chest as they travel along their path. They continue on and their wounds begin to heal. As the bleeding stops, these sufferers find they have come full circle, and they are stabbed again. The healing effort is lacerated, and the cycle begins anew. Health and wholeness are dashed. The hope of a new thing is unrealized. This is the hamster wheel. This is hell on earth.

I know the hamster wheel. To seek God when you are in hell and not be able to find him is the most despairing journey of the human heart. Many people in this situation use spiritual language to cover their cyclical wounds, desperately trying to hold on to some sense of meaning and purpose. I do not look down on their efforts to find God in the midst of crisis and difficulty. Even after leaving home and breathing a big sigh of relief, I continued to relive the chaos I had grown up with. It was all I knew.

But now I know there is a difference between suffering that is cyclical and destructive and suffering that is redemptive. I realize that distinguishing between types of suffering can lead us to a potential Pandora's box of questions about evil and suffering in the world. To answer these questions is not the intent of this book. Nor do I assume that these distinctions are prescriptive—set in stone. The distinctions I will be making are intended as general guidelines that can be applied practically so that people of God can be freed to recognize their purpose and not be shackled by endless patterns of futility and fear.

Throughout history the Enemy has used cyclical oppression to keep God's people enslaved, to keep them from recognizing the glorious purpose and hope to which they have been called. White slave owners in the Old South knew that once the African American slaves became educated, able to think and articulate their experiences, they would seek a higher form of life and recognize freedom as their inalienable right. So they passed laws forbidding anyone to teach slaves to read.

In the same way, if we stay blinded, uninformed and unable to understand or articulate what is happening to us, we cannot examine how our lives fall short of the glorious liberty we are entitled to as God's children. If we mistake the hamster wheel for God's will, we make God an oppressor rather than a libera-

tor, a justifier, an outrageous forgiver and the Author of life. To
live in freedom we must think intelligently about our lives and
stay open to the possibility that things may not be as predeter-
mined as we thought.

In the Gospels, Jesus does not succumb to every kind of suffering that comes his way. His identity as God's beloved Son and
his sense of purpose and calling cause him to avoid certain situations. God reminds him before he goes into the wilderness to
be tempted by the devil that Jesus is his beloved Son (Matthew
3:17). This reminder of his identity as the beloved one is to encourage Jesus and build him up before a period of desolation.
We too need to be reminded of who we are in the eyes of God.
Paul tells us that we are chosen by God (Colossians 3:12), his
"beloved children" (Ephesians 5:1).

In the wilderness, Jesus knows who he is. There is no doubt
in his mind—and he states it. The Enemy tries over and over to
challenge this identity. "If you are the Son of God, let's see you
prove it!" He distorts Scripture, and if Jesus were to follow what
Satan wanted, he would come under the bondage and oppression of evil. But he doesn't. Time after time he answers Satan's
distortions with statements of victory and purpose. When he
emerges from the wilderness, his identity leads him to begin his
ministry the right way. From the outset he tells people who he
is and why he has come. He reads from Isaiah:

> The Spirit of the Lord is upon me,
>   because he has anointed me
>   to bring good news to the poor.

He has sent me to proclaim release to the captives
>   and recovery of sight to the blind,
>   to let the oppressed go free,
>   to proclaim the year of the Lord's favor. (Luke 4:18-19)

This is who Jesus is—the liberator of captives and the champion of the oppressed. He states to the people that this is his mission and call. And at first they think he's great. But when he refers to incidents in Scripture in which God intervened on behalf of non-Jews (Luke 4:24-27), implying that God has sent him to the Gentiles, they bring him to a cliff and prepare to hurl him over. How quickly they change! What does Jesus do? Stand there and let himself be destroyed? Does he say, "It must be God's will that I suffer for what I said. Go ahead, guys. I'll die a martyr right now by letting you toss me over this ledge!"

No. Scripture tell us, "He passed through the midst of them and went on his way" (Luke 4:30). On his way to where? To fulfill the purpose for which he came. Immediately he starts healing people, setting them free. The people love him so much they try to keep him from leaving them (Luke 4:42), but Jesus is clear about his call. He responds, "I must proclaim the good news of the kingdom of God to the other cities also; for I was sent for this purpose" (Luke 4:43).

Would you be able to succinctly sum up your call and your reason for being sent to earth at this time? Are you able to spot scriptural distortions that perpetuate oppression rather than liberation? Are you able to act courageously and confidently in the truth that you have been beloved of God since the foundation of the world and are "of more value than many sparrows" (Matthew 10:31)? I know many Christians who don't feel worth one sparrow.

This book is about discovering your tremendous worth in Jesus Christ. It is meant to help you break out of the bondage that can steal your life and rob you of the purpose and call of God. In the following chapters I talk a lot about stopping the cyclical past in order to recognize God's liberation. The first crucial question to ask on this journey is, "Am I suffering because I am fulfilling my God-ordained call and purpose—or because I'm on a hamster wheel?" To help in the discernment process, I try to give practical suggestions and examples, not a list of self-help solutions. This book is an effort to help you get in step with the Holy Spirit, the only true Helper, and discern his direction for your life. I encourage you to read prayerfully and seek the Holy Spirit's transformation. Recognizing patterns, remembering who Jesus is and discovering the dreams God put deep inside you can open new channels for grace and change.

What I share with you on these pages is what I have lived. I am here now because of Jesus' love. Writing this book has made it necessary for me to turn myself inside out, exposing all my ragged edges and uneven seams. I have had to honestly examine the path my life has taken, including the many times my flaws and shortcomings got in the Lord's way. It has been necessary for me to assess what is holding me together these days and causing me to look forward to living rather than dying. So

I share with you my insights, reflections and stories in hope that they might shed some light on who God is and who we as God's people are called to be in Christ Jesus.

I start by describing the characteristics of hamster-wheel suffering, which we must recognize if we are going to be freed or help free those we love. The courage to change means we must dare to believe that although the hamster wheel is circling, there is a way out, a choice we can make that will launch us into a new way of living, loving and allowing ourselves to be loved.

2

Recognizing the Hamster Wheel

My marriage was a hamster-wheel marriage in which denial ran strong. We kept saying there was no problem. Our issues were a blip on the radar screen or a wrinkle in the fabric—but not a problem. I often didn't know where my husband, Tim, was for hours on end, we had heated arguments that were never resolved, and we failed to keep the promises we made each other—important promises. We were so fragmented and disorganized that the left hand didn't know what the right hand was doing. We didn't have many friends. Despite our dysfunction, I kept telling myself it wasn't so bad. And my life was still better than the craziness I had grown up with. I was trying so hard to hold everything together that I didn't see the patterns of my past emerging in my marriage. I thought I had gotten out. Instead I was repeating the old and familiar in a new way—and my marriage paid the price.

Realizing when we are in the hamster wheel is not easy. We

lose ourselves in the cycling and think we are actually going somewhere. But clear distinguishing markers can help us identify when we are running in endless circles and then we can make a plan to get out. Some of the characteristics of hamster-wheel suffering are outlined below.

HAMSTER-WHEEL SUFFERING IS SOLITARY

I have shared with you already that my family of origin functioned essentially in isolation from the outside world. This is often the case with abusive family systems. Many of the women I work with come to me because they are in abusive marriages, and isolation is a key weapon their abusers use to disempower them. I always try to link these women with a friend, a lay minister or a counselor. In relationship they are able to find validation for their feelings and begin to see beyond the enclosed world that has become their existence. It was in relationship with a friend that I found the courage to persevere when I made extremely painful but necessary changes. It was her encouragement and that of the church where she was associate pastor that helped me stay out of the hamster wheel.

The importance of being in community with other Christians is an essential part of discerning God's will for our life and following through on it. Community brings in the fresh aroma of new perspectives, ideas and alternatives. I was struck the other day, as I read the Scripture, that before the Holy Spirit came, the disciples were "all together in one place" (Acts 2:1). This "togetherness" was the church. When the Holy Spirit came, the tower of Babel was reversed. All the people heard the gospel in their own language, and God drew them together under a common vision and message. The church was created so that we do not need to be alone, feeling as though no one understands. In community, we can validate and discern as well as celebrate. If you are suffering alone without people around you who can share, pray and celebrate with you, it may be that you are in a hamster wheel. No hamster ever runs in his wheel with another hamster. It is a solo endeavor.

People in destructive cycles are afraid of relationships. Even if we are not forced into isolation by an abusive spouse, our tendency to isolate becomes more extreme the more we feel marginalized by our circumstances. Once we begin to see our situation as worse than everyone else's, once guilt and self-hate enter in, it becomes easy to convince ourselves that we don't fit in and that our suffering makes us different from others. Given these erroneous assumptions, why would we even try to connect with anyone on the outside?

When I had a pet hamster, it ran on its wheel at night— *squeak! squeak! squeak!* all evening long. Hamsters are nocturnal, becoming more active when the rest of the world is asleep. When it's us in the hamster wheel, the isolation we experience keeps us from seeing the light of day. Problems loom larger in our minds because we keep ourselves from others and don't benefit from their input—the light of their insight, so to speak.

One of our greatest sources of outreach at Menlo Park Presbyterian Church, where I am a pastor, is a divorce recovery ministry. It is a weekly gathering of men and women who come together to share the pain of recent (or not so recent) divorce or separation experiences. Unfortunately, many people feel ostracized by the church after the breakup of a marriage. I think of my Catholic friend who was so afraid she would be damned that it took all her courage just to come and see me. But with this group, I look around the room and see people in dialogue with one another. I see heads bowed in prayer, hands grasped in friendship, awareness of the need for God. Tears are shed, not in isolation but in the presence of others. This community buoys up, validates and confirms as well as teaches and corrects. Here is the church where people are "all together in one place," not just geographically, but psychologically and spiritually. It's a place where people recognize the frailty and brokenness of their own humanity, and unabashedly acknowledge their absolute dependence on God.

Isolation can be an attraction for many people who have been disappointed by others, abused or neglected. We might call these individuals "survivors." Survivors who have made it on their own find it difficult to ask others for help. Survivors find it challenging to trust and allow themselves to be cared for. Survivors can be great caregivers but not such great care receivers.

For a while I was in this category, going about my ministry with gusto. I couldn't receive in relationship; I could only give. And when you keep pouring a pitcher out onto dry ground, even if it's a pitcher with huge capacity, at some point that pitcher is going to dry up. I became aware through therapy that the care I was giving to others was really the care I wanted someone to give to me. Learning to receive in relationship with others has been a great source of strength for me and something I am still learning to do. It isn't easy. My tendency is to isolate, decide I don't need anyone, and wall others off when I am hurt or feeling blue. I know that this is not a healthy response, and after a time of being alone, I force myself to reach out. I do this because I know I need to trust and allow others to love and care for me even when I don't have it all together.

You get the sense from Paul, isolated in prison, that he longs for fellowship with others and that this longing comes from the core of his being. It is a passion, a deep desire, a gift from God. It isn't that he can't be alone. It's that the fellowship of believers gives him so much more joy and encouragement.

> I thank my God every time I remember you, constantly praying with joy in every one of my prayers for all of you, because of your sharing in the gospel from the first day until now. (Philippians 1:3-5)

> Therefore, my brothers and sisters, whom I love and long for, my joy and crown, stand firm in the Lord. (Philippians 4:1)

In order to be helped out of isolation into community, we need to have a desire and a willingness to receive in relationship. Receiving is core to the Christian message. We don't save ourselves. We receive or accept Christ into our lives. If we don't know how to receive from the brothers and sisters we can see, how can we hope to receive from a God we cannot see?

In his resurrection appearance, the very first thing Jesus asks his disciples to do is receive the Holy Spirit (John 20:22). In giving the Spirit he is breathing life on his disciples the same way he breathed life into Adam and Eve at the beginning of creation. He's telling them to open themselves up to taking in the life of his presence. To open themselves up to taking in good things and letting them stick. To open themselves up to trust, hope, forgiveness, a new way of being, a new creation.

Openness means vulnerability. That's what makes relationships a challenge for survivors. We might get hurt again. We might get lambasted, crushed or bruised. We've created good ways to avoid vulnerability, sheltering ourselves and not entering fully into a life of relationship. That's why the hamster wheel is attractive—it's a solo endeavor. That's why the "me and Jesus" motif is attractive—we leave God's people out of the picture. But Paul called the people of God the very body of Christ. Live in isolation from others, and you live not knowing the tangible presence of Christ on earth. A sign of health and of trust in God is to surrender enough to open up and receive strength from others, especially from God's people—the church.

HAMSTER-WHEEL SUFFERING IS DEPLETING

When I would watch our pet hamster, Nugget, run in his wheel, there was no doubt that he was getting a true little hamster workout. No one was making that wheel turn but him. If isolation is the first sign of hamster-wheel suffering, then Herculean effort is the second. It is necessary to put forth a tremendous amount of energy to keep things moving and perpetuate the destructive cycle. The rhythmic lull of life as we know it, as we have always known it, keeps us running in the wheel when we ought to let it stop.

"I have to stay with him," a woman told me recently. "I have to stay because my pastor told me that if I left I would be disobeying God, and I wouldn't go to heaven. He told me that I am probably not the wife I should be, and that's why my husband beats me. Besides, if I left it would destroy my husband's Christian witness. He's an evangelist, you know. I think I just need to try harder to be a good wife."

This is an extreme example of hamster-wheel suffering. This woman lived an isolated life with no transportation and no outlets for herself. She was making a Herculean effort to please. She was constantly trying harder—to not burn the roast, to keep the children tidy and quiet. It was amazing she had made it to my office at all.

"It will happen again," I told her. "There will always be something wrong. No matter how hard you try, you will not be able to please him. You've got to get out of there."

She didn't believe me. She shook her head, and I think she thought I was terribly un-Christian to suggest such a thing. Six months later she was back. Nothing had worked. Eventually, with some encouragement and a concrete plan put into place with the help of some wonderful women at our church, she found freedom from the abusive cycle. Now she sits with other women and uses her experience to free them from the pain of abuse. If she had kept trying on her own steam to keep the wheel turning, she probably would not be alive today. If her husband had not killed her, she would have collapsed either emotionally or physically from sheer exhaustion.

One of the things I ask people I perceive to be in the hamster wheel is how they're doing physically. Often the stress of running around and around, going nowhere, has taken its toll on their limbs, joints and organs. No one can sustain continued grief, pain, stress and trauma without physical effects. Nor is it God's will that anyone be destroyed by their circumstances. But if you don't stop the wheel from turning, if you don't give up the solo show of holding everything together, gradually you will be destroyed.

When I was a child, I felt even at a young age that I had to hold it together for my parents. As a result I was sick all the time. Allergies, strep throat and chronic ear infections plagued me. Our family doctor would look at me and shake his head, saying, "I sure wish I could give you a new nose." My nose was stuffed up all the time. By the time I was an adult the pattern of chronic sickness was ingrained. Feeling exhausted and depleted was part of life.

"I just can't do it anymore," people often tell me. "But if I don't keep going, everything will fall apart." Sometimes it's just fine to let things fall apart—before *you* do—because then it becomes possible to rebuild.

There are a hundred and one reasons we can give for why we must keep the hamster wheel turning. "It wouldn't be good for the kids." "There's not enough money." "What will people think?" "I can't change my life—it's chaotic enough as it is." These cycles of thinking rob us of the energy we need to go in a new direction, the energy to discover God's call and purpose for our lives.

Stopping the hamster wheel can be painful, much the way hitting bottom is painful for an alcoholic. Our joints may ache. Our lives may feel empty without all the frenetic activity. There's no doubt that getting out of the wheel takes courage. It requires a stalwart trust that God will see us through the lonely, unfamiliar times and provide the deep healing we crave at the center of our being.

If you are depleted at the end of each day and wake in the morning with little capacity to enjoy or anticipate, chances are you are running in that rodent wheel. With the help of others and with Jesus holding your hand, you can take a leap of faith and get out.

HAMSTER-WHEEL SUFFERING GOES NOWHERE

When we're in the hamster wheel, we continually find ourselves right back where we started. This is obvious to the outside observer—anyone can tell you the hamster ends up in the same place he was when he began. But it's not so obvious to us. We think we're being diligent and intense in our endurance of difficulty, but in the end we go absolutely nowhere.

The Enemy loves distortion, and if he can get us to think that we're going somewhere for the kingdom of God when we're actually going nowhere at all, he has successfully distracted us from the reason we were created: to glorify God and enjoy him forever.

If we assume that all suffering is constructive and fail to discern that we are in a self-destructive cycle, we risk missing out on God's plan to give us a "future with hope" (Jeremiah 29:11)—a plan that takes us somewhere. Again, Jesus didn't succumb to every kind of suffering. When that mob of angry people tried to push him off the cliff, he passed through them and went on his way. Jesus knew that his life would eventually be sacrificed, but the time was not now.

It may be hard for us to come to terms with the reality that we are going nowhere. It may seem to us, as we are caught up in the dizzying frenzy of the hamster wheel, that we are making great progress. This often happens to people we might consider to be very successful. One high-level corporate executive told me, "I made it to the top, and found there was nothing there."

The longing of our lives, deep at the core, has nothing to do with self-made success. It has everything to do with finding our God-given call: our divinely appointed reason for being in the world.

(3)

A Gracious Intrusion

As I have shared with you, my early family life made me question whether I had a purpose or call at all. I wondered why I was alive. I thought about killing myself often, and my mood was flat and depressed.

As a teenager, I was headed south. I wanted to believe in God, but I had been told many times that God was out to get me, and my image of him was distorted by false language that made his nature murky and frightening. One afternoon when I was thirteen, I was feeling desperate and alone. My parents had separated, and my mother had whisked my sister and me across the country to a new school in the middle of the year.

Without the fragments of my father's love and concern, I was in a deep depression. I was failing science in an unfamiliar school. I was convinced I was fat and ugly. And I had just found out that my parents had given my dog away. I loved that sheltie, and the rage and sorrow that welled up in me after overhearing the news (no one told me directly) took the last teaspoon of pluck out of me. Sitting on the couch in the living room I began to cry. This in itself was not unusual, but this time I couldn't stop. It was as if I was being sucked down into an abyss. I was out of strength and didn't have one bit of tenacity left.

The truth is that so often when we are at our lowest ebb, when we have nothing left, it seems to oil the hinges for the door of God's presence to swing magnificently wide, allowing us to experience the reality of God's presence in a whole new way. For me, in that moment on the couch, the song "Amazing Grace" crackling out over the radio, sung by the old-time voice of George Beverly Shea, oiled those hinges. What I experienced as I only half-listened to the familiar hymn hit me broadside. It pulled me up and caught me by surprise. It stopped my tears, but then started them again for an entirely different reason. I was overcome with the presence of Jesus.

As I sat there, I was flooded with a delighted, almost chuckling love that rippled through my being like a river. Wave after wave of it poured through me; I couldn't stop it. I had the sense that the joy and warmth and aliveness was endless and that I was eternally held in that reality. This was not the God I knew, the one who was distant, disapproving and coercive, the one who chewed people up and spit them out. This was a God who longed to be in relationship with me. I had the sense that I was known, that my name was acknowledged, that this Someone who knew me (did I dare call this One by that awful name— God?), had allowed my life to have meaning. I wasn't a forgotten bit of froth tossed up by a wave and left to evaporate on the sand. In the loving gaze of this Someone, I was an eternal being who was infinitely more important and valuable than I had ever believed.

That night I stayed up all night and read Scripture. The words jumped off the page and walked around with new life. I was transfixed by the fact that as I read the Bible I no longer felt condemned but outrageously and fervently cared for. This was a love that any human love I had experienced up to that point couldn't even begin to approach. Even at forty-eight years old, when I go back to that moment, it defines who God is for me.

I told this story once in a sermon and was jolted by the responses of the people after the service. I must have heard similar accounts at least ten times over the course of three services that morning. With tears in their eyes, people said things like, "I know what you mean. When I was very young I had an experience of Jesus' love, and I've never forgotten it. Life has been hard, but I keep remembering Jesus' love—the way I experienced him back then." The magnificence of Jesus' presence is unforgettable. It touches everything we long for as humans. You don't forget Jesus' presence. You can't.

When I was young, I lived in Switzerland for a year with my family. If you followed the road we lived on up the hill, you would come to a large field along one side. The villagers who lived in that area told us that, on a clear day, there was a magnificent view of Mount Blanc across this field. Mount Blanc was the highest of the Swiss Alps, but try as we might, we couldn't catch a glimpse of it. Every time we drove up there, the mist hung low and the clouds were heavy, and all we saw was an empty field. After a while we stopped journeying that way, thinking that perhaps the view was overrated, an exaggeration meant to trick naïve Americans into renting houses close by.

But then one day early in the morning, we traveled up that hill again. This time the mists were gone—and there the mountain stood. A great jagged peak was soaring up to the sky, flashing reds and pinks from the rising sun. It was glorious, and we marveled. We made many more travels to that field after that, and most of the time the view was obstructed by mist. But we had seen that alpine giant once and the vision stayed with us. Occasionally it greeted us again with grandeur, but even when we couldn't see it, we knew it was there.

Many people have had an experience of God's presence, and they know he is there. Sometimes they are estranged from him for a long time, but they come back to him—they come back because they remember. They remember when the mist lifted, when they knew Jesus was real, when the reality of his presence was so magnificent that it stuck.

One man shared with me that he'd had a grandmother who rocked him to sleep at night, singing "Jesus Loves Me," when he was three years old. He had become a successful man, competent in every way the world deems important. Yet he remembered his grandmother singing to him in the cauldron of an argumentative, atheistic home with parents who told him God was a crutch. "I felt God's presence," he said. "As she sang, I was aware that there was something more than this life." This experience eventually brought him back to church in his forties, with his own children in tow.

When God's presence enters our meager four-score-and-ten existence, as we hack it out by the sweat of our brow, it is something we remember for the rest of our days. It resonates with the deepest part of who we are, because it is what we were created for. It chimes out, "The one who is in you is greater than the one who is in the world" (1 John 4:4). It is a vital reference point in our spiritual walk, and it keeps refreshing us and bringing us new life. This gracious intrusion into the way we think, the way we live, the way we create our world pulls us out of our distorted thinking and brings new life to the way we describe God.

I get criticized for being a grace fanatic. I get pinned to the wall at times by those who think I spend too much time talking about the love of God. I can't help it. It's all I know. I was rescued from hell on earth, from atheism, from suicide, by this Eternal Lover, and to not talk about it would be disastrous. To go back to being motivated by fear, by works, by climbing a ladder to try to please God with my filthy-rags righteousness would be a slap in the face to the One who calls me to live from a place of gratitude, forgiveness and adoration of Jesus.

Do you see how the wrong kinds of spiritual language can distort the image of God and make it difficult to get out of the hamster wheel? This is why we have so many joyless Christians walking around. They've forgotten who God is! They've forgot-

ten or have never known "the deep, deep love of Jesus, vast, un-
measured, boundless, free," as the old song puts it. They've
been duped by angry preachers, condemning parents or the
critically spiritual who point out weaknesses in others for their
own self-aggrandizement.

The wrong kinds of spiritual language create horrible idola-
tries, which we worship without even realizing it. Our image of
God, the picture we have of him, is vital for our freedom in
Christ. It is vital for our joy in Christ. It is vital for getting out
of the hamster wheel. Ask yourself, "Am I worshiping the God
of Jesus Christ, or am I worshiping some other god that was
created in my own mind by legalism or punishment?"

Until we are transformed by the Holy Spirit our tendency is
to create God in our own image based on past experiences, human interactions and our horizontal world. The Israelites made
the golden calf by melting their jewelry. They created an idol
from the stuff of their lives. They made it from what they had
acquired in the world. What did they come up with? A cow!
Moo. Couldn't they have come up with something a little more
transcendent? If you are going to make an idol, folks, at least do
something inspiring.

But we are no better. When we create God from the stuff of
our experiences in this world, when we melt together a con-
glomerate of what we accumulate in this life, we are bound to
come up with a pretty sorry representation of God. That is why
preachers and teachers and all Christian leaders must use language that adequately expresses who God is in the person of

Jesus Christ. Jesus is called the Word of God. He is the divine
expression of love poured out lavishly without limit. He is the
very essence of God's heart. He is the eternal transcendent one
who is without end in his mercy and compassion and ebullient,
self-sustaining, resurrection joy. The words we use can remind
us again and again of this truth. "The truth will make you free,"
Jesus tells his disciples (John 8:32). And what is truth? To know
God and his Son, Jesus Christ. The knowledge of God's nature
in its wonderful reality can free us from the shackles of idolatry.

A look at the Gospels reveals that Jesus had tremendous dis-
taste for the ways the words of Scripture were used to validate
oppression and human suffering. Look at what he does with the
interpretation of "Remember the sabbath day, and keep it holy"
(Exodus 20:8). He goes out and heals people on the Sabbath,
setting them free from illness and disability—to the chagrin of
the scribes and Pharisees (John 7). He wasn't supposed to do
that! But I can just see Jesus shaking his head in frustration.
"This law was made for you! You weren't made to keep this
law!" The dos and don'ts of Scripture are meant for freedom,
not for hamster-wheel futility.

Jesus' ministry was focused on undoing the misinterpreta-
tion of Scripture. The disciples stand by, wide-eyed, and stam-
mer, "But . . . but . . . you're not supposed to do that!" The Pharisees are even more surprised—and outraged. "You're not
supposed to heal on the Sabbath, or set that prostitute free. The
law says she has to be stoned. You aren't supposed to care about
Samaritans or touch lepers. The words in the law say they are

unclean! You aren't supposed to say that you are God—that's blasphemy!"

God's Word made flesh was a profound revelation that we had managed to use to distort God and keep people in bondage, running around in a hamster wheel, serving a God made up of our own stuff and in our own image.

From Exodus to Revelation God is constantly appearing to set his people free. Look! You're not slaves anymore; here's the Promised Land. Look! You've got Jesus; here I am to die for you so you don't have to sacrifice anymore. Look! Here's the Holy Spirit to empower you to live in freedom. Look! Someday I will set things right, and there will be no more suffering and sighing. Don't succumb to legalism—a system based on fear. Don't let laws be your security; instead let my love keep you safe, secure and liberated.

In the Sermon on the Mount, Jesus declares, "You have heard that it was said . . . but I say to you . . ." (Matthew 5:21-43). Jesus is declaring his divinity by rewriting the Mosaic law. He is calling people to conform to a pattern of grace and freedom, which was the intent of the law to begin with.

Since so much of Jesus' ministry was focused on reinterpreting the intent of the words of Scripture, redefining our image of God and helping people to see that "God so loved the world," it seems that the church ought to sit up and take notice. How does spiritual language create a distorted image of God and keep us in the hamster wheel?

In the next chapter we will learn to recognize the symptoms

of hamster-wheel language. Recognizing this language can help set us free. But the ultimate healing power comes from an experience of God's presence. After my own miraculous encounter with the love of Jesus, my struggles were far from over. The difference, however, was that I knew who God was, and I could keep going back to that liberating experience again and again as a reference point. I could begin to believe that I was loved and that maybe, even for me in the dark tunnel of my childhood, there was a future and a hope.

(4)

How False Spirituality Keeps Us Stuck

The language we use creates much of the reality in which we live. Language expresses our state of mind, and when we share it, it shapes another person's state of mind. Just as God created the world through his word, so our words create our world. The difference is that God's words create only life and beauty because God is all good. We, on the other hand, have the capacity to create both life and death with our words. We can destroy others with our words.

Words were a big deal in my family growing up, often used to tear down rather than build up. Some people ask incredulously why I am still a Christian, and I agree that given the past distortions of faith I experienced, I shouldn't be. For a while, as a preteen, I decided I didn't believe in God. I wanted to get out and stay out of all that nonsense. God seemed to operate the way my family did—with the chewing gum approach. Chew on people for a while to experience all their flavor and consistency, and then, once you've depleted them of taste and elasticity, spit them into the trash can.

My image of God was created by words that motivated me to respond to God out of fear. "If you don't comply with my wishes and demands, God will not bless you," I heard again and again. "God told me that you have evil thoughts in your heart toward me. No one who has evil thoughts toward me will escape God's judgment." If something good happened to me, I was told, "Beware when all men speak well of you," and "The first shall be last." These words terrified me. Who would want to have anything to do with God after such messages of gloom? Thank goodness for my experience of Jesus' love. This gracious intrusion into the abusive cycle redefined everything.

The wrong kind of spiritual language can keep us stuck in the hamster wheel a long time. It can produce feelings of guilt, obligation and shame that distort the image of God. We can use it to protect ourselves when we don't want to get in touch with our pain. Sometimes we don't know what to do, so instead of being honest, we resort to lingo that is safe and familiar. Following are some types of spiritual language that keep us from being genuine with ourselves and others, that keep us from recognizing our call and purpose, and most importantly, that keep us distant from who we are and who God is.

THE LANGUAGE OF DENIAL

Spiritual language can be used to help us deny that a problem exists. Denial is a fine mode of protection. It keeps pain out of our mind. It holds at bay what we do not wish to remember. It is a survivor's shield that we can hold in front of our faces to block our view of the horrific landscape around us.

People often talk about denial in a condescending way, as if it were something to be ridiculed. But denial has helped me cope at certain points in my past. There is a strong benefit to defenses that preserve our sanity; sometimes confronting an issue head-on would wreck us emotionally. There is a time to be in denial, but there is also a time to work through the pain little by little, as much as we can handle at any one time. Once we name the problem, we are ready to get off the hamster wheel.

Denial was a prime tool that I used to stay on the hamster wheel even after I was married. Since my mother's problems hadn't been owned or recognized, I found it difficult to own or recognize that Tim and I had problems. The first step to getting off the hamster wheel is acknowledging that you even have a problem. I wasn't able to do this for a long time. I didn't want to look at the pain in my past or acknowledge my present relational mess. I wasn't even sure I had permission to call it bad. What if there was no problem? What if it was just in my head? Or what if I was exaggerating an issue that was no big deal?

I once sat with someone who had lost a loved one. She kept saying, "God works all things together for good," and the spiritual lingo helped her to be present in a situation that was so painful she could hardly bear it. After our first meeting, I finally said, "You know, it's awful that your loved one died. It must be very hard for you to pray right now. Why don't you let me do your praying for a while?" At this point the woman burst into tears. Gently we began to talk about the grief and loss that was just under the surface.

Many of us use spiritual lingo to remain in denial so that everything stays fine, shallow and nice. The church can be a perpetrator of the fine, the shallow and the nice; our hollow spiritual language acts as a gloss that covers the ugly stuff. Perhaps one of the reasons churches breed this kind of coping strategy is that we feel have to defend God when something bad happens. Admitting the anguish that we feel might mean that God is not faithful.

It's funny that we do this in churches, because the Bible doesn't sugarcoat things at all. It is ruthlessly honest, raw and real. When the psalmist is in trouble, instead of saying, "Well, all things work together for good," he cries out with despair. "Will the Lord reject forever? / Will he never show his favor again?" (Psalm 77:7 NIV). "My heart is in anguish within me" (Psalm 55:4 NIV). "My God, my God, why have you forsaken me? / Why are you . . . so far from the words of my groaning?" (Psalm 22:1 NIV). "How can I go on? Why do you let terrible things happen to the people you love?" he asks God. This kind of honesty testifies to a relationship with God that's so strong it doesn't need to be protected. God holds on to us and preserves us. We do not preserve God.

THE LANGUAGE OF MINIMIZATION

The language of minimization is something we use to neutralize the negative charge of an oppressive hamster-wheel situation. "It's not so bad," we tell ourselves. Churches are rife with this kind of thinking because many of them teach, directly or indirectly, that Christians shouldn't have problems—if they do, somehow it's their own fault. God ought to be enough. If they had more faith, prayed more regularly or memorized more Scripture, their problems would vanish. In order for these people to feel that they are good Christians, they must minimize their issues and keep them insignificant in their mind.

Nowhere in Scripture do we see someone praying to God and God telling them, "It's no big deal. Buck up and stop whining." In fact, Jesus speaks about how God clothes the lilies, cares even about what we wear and eat, and considers each day of our lives important (Matthew 6:28; Luke 12:27).

Children know this instinctively. Their smallest concerns get shot up to God in prayer at bedtime. "Graham was mean to me." "I lost my hamster, please help me find him." "Give me a friend." "Help there not be peanut butter for lunch." Jesus said that God cares even when a sparrow dies and that he loves us far more than the birds (Matthew 10:31). What happens to us, what causes us pain, is held much more closely to God's heart than we know. Nothing is minimized in God's economy.

But minimization can escalate out of control when problems are immense and we simply don't know how to deal with them. This kind of coping occurred in the following interaction I had with a man, Rod, who wanted to talk about a situation. Rod kept telling me it was "nothing." See what you think.

"Well, here I am," Rod said as he came in the door. "I finally got in the office to see you. I'm sure you have a lot of other people to see, so I'm sorry to take up your time."

"It's time that I had set aside for you," I said. "I'm glad you're here, and I have almost an hour for us to talk. How are you doing?"

"I don't have to take long. I just wanted to let you know that I have lymphoma. I mean, it's nothing new. I've had it for a long time but now it's stage four and I'm feeling a little depressed. I'd just like a quick prayer."

"That's terrible. I am so sorry."

"Yeah, well, as I said, it's been a long road. Nothing new."

"I bet. Did you know we have a men's cancer support group that meets here? It's a bunch of guys that get together, pray and talk through what it's like to have a long-term disease that can make you feel sick for extended periods of time."

"Well, it's not that I can't deal with it. I mean, I think of all the poverty in the world, and people who are really suffering. My mother had a bad liver and a heart problem. My brother, well, he's been divorced and has an addiction problem. I'm happily married, have two great kids, and I've had a good life so far. I'm grateful for that. And I feel guilty for feeling depressed and lethargic when I may not have that much longer to . . . be around."

I looked at him and for a moment we were silent.

"It is not a small matter to be in stage four cancer," I finally said. "This *is* a big deal. You've got a lot of concerns inside that you may want to talk about. I can't even imagine the turmoil you must be in. Are you concerned for your wife? For your kids?"

This comment was all he needed. Rod nodded, choked up and began to tell me what was really going on. He felt abandoned by God. He didn't like being sick. He wanted to be healed. He thought that by not making a "big deal" of things he was having faith and that this would ensure his healing. He was also lonely. We had a good talk and a long, heartfelt prayer. He agreed to go to the support group. He would also get prayer from a team designed to pray for healing. I offered him some other counseling options as well.

Minimization of his problem was a way for Rod to cope with the overwhelming sorrow of his situation and the worry that his illness might separate him from his wife and children. It was necessary for him to keep the brutal reality at arm's length just so he could function. And by trying not to dwell on the underside of things, Rod thought he was having more faith and perhaps would be more likely to experience healing. But all this minimization was masking an intense desperation in Rod's heart and preventing him from receiving the support and understanding he needed.

I find it interesting when I read Scripture to note that when Jesus commends people by saying, "Your faith has made you whole," he doesn't equate the word *faith* with the ability of people to minimize a problem. Actually, the people Jesus commends are those who are doing precisely the opposite. They *know* they have a big problem, and because they know it, they make great efforts to reach out to Jesus. Like the woman with the flow of blood, who is well aware that Jesus is the only one who can help her. No minimization here, just honest human desperation. As people acknowledge their weakness and dependency, Jesus meets them.

I see minimization often with spouses who live in violent situations, like the woman who said to me, point blank, "Well, it's only the first time he's pulled the phone out of the wall and broken a window. He's under a lot of stress at work. It's not like he curses at the children all the time. It's really not so bad."

Jesus never minimizes. He sees the cruelty of the world, and he feels the pain of others deeply. He cries at Lazarus' tomb (John 11:35). He invites people who are "weary and carrying heavy burdens" to come to him (Matthew 11:28), and he has compassion on those who are like "sheep without a shepherd" (Matthew 9:36). He calls our generation "faithless and perverse" (Matthew 17:17) and anguishes over going to the cross because he knows how hellish it will be to feel the weight of the sins of the world on his shoulders. He is, according to Isaiah, "a man of suffering and acquainted with infirmity" (Isaiah 53:3). Brennan Manning says, in *The Ragamuffin Gospel*,

> When we speak of Jesus Christ as Emmanuel, God with us, we are saying that the greatest lover in history knows what hurts us. Jesus reveals a God who is not indifferent to human agony, a God who fully embraces the human condition and plunges into the thick of our human strug-

gle. There is nothing Jesus does not understand about the heartache that hangs like a cloud over the valley of history. In His own being He feels every separation and loss, every heart split open with grief, every cry of mourning down the corridors of time.

If Jesus felt the rawness of humanity and cried out, "My God, my God, why have you forsaken me?" then certainly we too can have confidence that coming face to face with our own sorrow is a part of life, a part of healing, a part of being genuine and honest before God. God knows our hearts and sees beneath our coping strategies to the raw pain there. Perhaps by becoming more honest with ourselves we draw nearer to the mind of Christ.

LANGUAGE THAT FORCES AN OPPOSITE REACTION

I have just a brief word here. We use opposite-reaction language when we decide that God, or people, or the Bible will not allow us to feel a certain way. "I'm not supposed to feel bad, so I'm going to feel good," we say, putting all the energy we want to use to kick the dog into petting the dog instead. The dog is still ticking us off, but we simply flip a switch and make ourselves act the opposite of how we feel.

This kind of language was rampant in the seventies with a Christian movement that declared that no matter what happened, all we had to do was "praise the Lord." If we did, everything would work out all right. Many churches still promote this perspective in varying degrees. If we "stay positive" some-how we can then control God with our great faith. The Bible does say to rejoice in all circumstances (Philippians 4:4), but it also says to "weep with those who weep" (Romans 12:15). A forced positive response works for a while, but eventually the ugly stuff seeps out in other ways. Faith is a gift, not a way to force a desired outcome.

THE LANGUAGE OF AVOIDANCE

I remember sitting with a woman whom I absolutely wanted to throttle. (I realize that this is not exactly a pastoral attitude.) I cared deeply for this woman and wanted to see her get her life on track, but she kept using spiritual lingo to keep herself safe and distant from what was really going on. The lingo allowed her to avoid getting the help she needed, and it was clear from my standpoint that she was close to a nervous breakdown. Our conversation went something like this.

"Jenny, I'd like to refer you to a counselor who is a wonderful person, whom I deeply respect, and who will be able to help you work through some of the things you've shared with me to-day."

"I've already been to counseling. I know what they say, and they don't help. I've read a bunch of books, but they don't help either. It's only the Lord who can help."

"That's for sure. God is the only one who can really help, and in a minute we'll pray and ask for help. But sometimes we need someone with 'skin on' to sort out the pain of our past. It's not head knowledge that we're after, here; I think you need heart knowledge of what you already know in your head."

"Well, God has told me that I don't need counseling. All I need to do is pray. I'm signing up for this Christian conference on prayer. I think it's what the Lord wants me to do."

She patted a brochure and nodded as if to reassure herself that she had the answer.

"I think it will be a good conference, and I hope you get a lot out of it," I responded, trying to affirm her effort. I knew it was hard for her to take initiative. "But I know you go to a lot of conferences and you hear a lot of really good speakers. Somewhere all this good stuff is getting lost in the transfer because you still aren't able to live the way you want to live—the way the speakers tell you how you are 'supposed' to live, and life still is very burdensome for you."

Jenny shifted uneasily in her chair and got a little teary.

"It is very hard," she mumbled.

Oh, good. We're finally getting somewhere, I thought.

"But," she said, looking up at me suddenly with a smile as glossy as the brochure she was holding, "I'm fine. Jesus said, 'Ask and you will receive,' and that is what I am going on. I don't need anyone. All I need is the Lord."

"Jenny," I tried one last time. "The Lord has given us one another to help us get through the hard times. And by the looks of it, you are going through a pretty hard time right now."

"So did a lot of people in the Bible. 'Blessed are you who are persecuted for righteousness' sake,'" she declared like a little parrot. "Well, that's what it is. I am being persecuted and no one understands this unless they are spiritually minded. Someday I'm going to get my reward and that's what I'm waiting for."

I prayed with Jenny. I continue to pray for her. As the years have come and gone, Jenny has stayed immobilized. She hasn't changed. I see her cycle in and out of episodic depression. I see her looking blankly at me during worship. I see her alone, her hair greasy, her clothes disheveled.

In contrast, there are some in our church who readily admit that they suffer from a mental illness. It is healing for me to work with people who are honest about their difficulties. Accurately naming the problem has helped them live their lives with an openness and vulnerability that invites others into their experience. They have formed a fellowship group called HELP (healing, encouragement, love and prayer) with more than two hundred people on the mailing list. HELP meets once a week to share a meal, have devotions and most of all pray for one another. I have never seen such fervent prayers. These people don't need a curriculum. They don't need cutesy gimmicks to keep them interested. All they want to do is pray, and it is to them that I give urgent prayer requests when I have them.

Many of the folks who struggle with mental illness have unabashedly declared their utter dependence on God. One woman in particular has testified in church how Jesus was present with her in the midst of a hospitalization for clinical depression. She saw Jesus walking her out of darkness and bringing her into a lighter place. "I still struggle," she said to the four thousand people who came to worship that weekend. "I know I am weak. But God is my strength."

The honesty of her testimony was a tribute to the HELP group. They had made church a safe place in which to share truthfully that Jesus was present in the thick of emotional pain. This language was healing language. It opened the door for several people to come to HELP when they had previously been too ashamed to admit their problem. I also received several phone calls from people whose children suffered with bipolar disorder and who were grateful that we had addressed mental illness in the services.

People come from all over to an annual conference sponsored by the HELP ministry to discuss the importance of community and to learn how to incorporate those with mental illnesses into the life of the church. These people faithfully show up for one another week after week, year after year. They remember birthdays, they celebrate small victories, they don't hold back on congratulating one another. People who support those with mental illnesses are also included in the fellowship. It helps these copers to hear what supporters go through and vice versa. Open communication like this has been pivotal in facilitating trust and stamping out stigma.

The HELP group knows that avoidance is a pattern that can grow like a malignancy. The more you avoid, the less and less you see, and problems create more problems when they are not addressed. Larger and thicker blinders are necessary to continue the avoidance pattern. For instance, many people tell me they are holding their marriage together for the sake of the children, because the Bible tells them to do it. But they also confide that there is no marriage to speak of; there is nothing that makes living with their spouse joyful, uplifting or supportive. For years they have tried to "make it work" and have avoided marital counseling. They have been too ashamed to share their marital issues with friends so that they can receive prayer and support. They would rather go it alone.

Now, I am a marriage proponent. I am *for* doing everything in your power to work out your relationship. Tim and I are living proof that if you hang on by the skin of your teeth, you can indeed work it out. We had to rebuild from scratch, and we are a different couple than we were twelve years ago. However, sometimes people would rather hang on to the shambles—walk on loose floorboards, step over rusty nails and tape over shattered windows—than get out the scaffolding to rebuild. Sometimes I try to wake folks up by saying, "So you're a hypocrite then?"

"What do you mean?" they respond, taken aback.

"Well, you're preserving the external show when internally there is nothing there. Jesus called hypocrites whitewashed tombs."

"But God hates divorce."

"Precisely," I will say. "God hates it when love goes stale, our hearts are broken by each other and promises go by the wayside. It sounds to me like you are already divorced in spirit. No sharing. No love. No intimacy. God looks on the heart. A divorce is just a piece of paper that states what often is the case already."

"But the Bible says I'm supposed to submit," many women will say.

"The Bible also says that your husband is supposed to love you the way Christ loved the church," I answer (see Ephesians 5:22-28). "How did Christ love his people? He suffered and died. He told them how much he loved them, he forgave them when they messed up, he encouraged them, he wanted them with him, and he endorsed them as friends and ambassadors. It's easy to give yourself over to someone who loves you that much because he is giving himself to you in turn. This is a love relationship—the essence of marriage. I suggest that if you don't want this marriage to end in divorce—on paper, even though it seems you're already living it—that you get help. Work it through. Hammer it out. Get real, and get going."

If you're struggling with your marriage relationship, don't avoid the problem any longer. Call the dry bones what they really are. Say it like it is! Dry bones have been known to rise again.

THE LANGUAGE OF RATIONALIZATION

If we can think about a situation in a way that helps us wrap our mind around it, it can definitely be helpful. But when our thinking becomes a way to distance ourselves from our feelings, we need to pause and take stock of our internal state.

"I've lost everything," someone recently confided in me. "My house, my family, my job—gone. But God wanted it this way, so that's it. All my days were planned ahead of time, the Scripture says. I've just got to realize that God's will must be done."

Well, this is all too slick and too quick. It's like wallpapering a room when the plaster is crumbling underneath. Slap on a Scripture! Slap on a happy face! Presto—the room is done. The building is falling apart, but it sure looks pretty.

God conveniently gets blamed for a lot of things that are not his will at all. Rationalizing is a process where we come up with reasons that justify actions or consequences that are often the cause of our own poor choices. God is an easy target. If we can blame God rather than making clear distinctions and perhaps some difficult decisions we can stay "stuck in the muck" of our own inertia—our hamster-wheel process. Rationalizing also distances us from our emotions and from an honest relationship with others and with God.

CONCLUSION

Language—the words we use—are vitally important. Jesus, the living Word, was full of grace and truth. Truth includes the pain of this world—combined with grace that assures us that the reality of resurrection life is bigger than the worst that evil can do. Grace and truth belong together. Without truth—honesty with ourselves, others and God—we will lapse into one form or another of the hamster-wheel language described in this chapter. We will find ourselves going nowhere, unable to articulate or come to terms with our own brokenness and need for God. Without grace, however, honesty gets us nowhere, except to perpetuate human despair. Grace enters in through the words of Jesus that bring forgiveness and the promised Holy Spirit to us—and the cry for this forgiveness comes to us from the depths of Jesus' pain on a cross. These words promise us a resurrection morning, the healing of our brokenness and a chance to stop running in circles.

The Blame Game

People in AA have a special term for the way we revert to thought patterns that keep us trapped on the hamster wheel: They call it "stinking thinking." Two patterns of stinking thinking seem particularly operative in Christian culture. Both have to do with blame and judgment rather than grace and truth.

RIGID THINKING

Once couples have children, they often return to the church even if they don't have a personal faith of their own. They do this because they want their children to be "good people" and learn moral values. They want their kids to know what's right and wrong. And there's nothing wrong with that. It's a good thing to want children to be trained properly.

But going to church just for the sake of moral values is limited in scope and dimension, and it won't last. It's like expecting cut flowers to look nice longer than a week or two. Cut off from the source of life—the God who wants us to live our lives out of love for him—moral values wither and die. Ultimately, worthwhile values must spring out of our love for Jesus. Gradually, as a result of spending time with him, we begin to live as he did. Not because we're trying hard but because the Holy Spirit produces the fruit of God in us. This process pulls the Christian life out of the realm of dos and don'ts and into the realm of a love relationship with God that is intricately connected to everyday life.

A harsh "moral values" mindset is an example of the kind of thinking that sacrifices people to principle. I find that people use rigid thinking as a way to make complicated problems simple. Many people who are extremely rigid in how they come across have huge internal struggles with immoral thoughts and actions. They appeal to a black and white model of thought to try to keep themselves in line with what they believe God wants.

However, this kind of simplistic thinking doesn't translate effectively to the complexity of life and the depth of what it means to be a human being. The truth is that Jesus lived in the gray. He loved to hang in the murky backwater of life— with the outcasts and sinners. He did ascribe to certain standards of behavior, which we would find life-giving to ascribe to as well. But in the gray of life, we in our limited earthly scope can be hard-pressed to tell which people are "good" and which are "bad."

Do we have a spiritual telescope that can look into the hearts of everyone and categorize them like species of ants? This one goes in the righteous pile. This one gets damned. This one has done some awful things but says she's sorry, so she's OK. This one isn't sorry but ought to be, so he gets scratched off the list. Obviously there are no such definitive distinctions. Do we even know when someone accepts Christ whether he or she has done it from the heart? We can hope that it is so, but we never know for sure.

"Not everyone who says to me, 'Lord, Lord,' will enter the kingdom of heaven," Jesus told the people (Matthew 7:21). We aren't the ones commissioned to separate the sheep from the goats. That's what God does, and his mercy is beyond our comprehension. It isn't our position to figure it out. Our rigid structures, inflexible critiques and strict formulas cannot hope to match up with the intricacies of human life. Only God, who sees the heart, is judge. Thank God it's God! "We have not been given the authority to judge," Pentecostal minister David du Plessis said years ago. "We have only been given the authority to forgive."

This is where our right-and-wrong abstractions butt heads with specific individuals and circumstances—with real life. If Jesus had been worried about the moral values of his time he never would have associated with tax collectors and sinners. He never would have healed non-Jews or saved a prostitute's life when the law dictated that she be destroyed. Jesus said, "What I speak . . . I speak just as the Father has told me" (John 12:50). He said nothing about moral values—ever. He said everything about his relationship with God.

PROJECTIVE THINKING

When you go to a cinema, the movie projector takes what is inside of it and projects it out onto the screen. You hardly think about the mechanism behind you. Rather, your focus is elsewhere. This is what happens in relational projection as well.

Projection is essentially putting onto another person or institution all the bad things (or good things) that you don't want to acknowledge as your own. Often the church is a target for projection when people are angry at God about something difficult in their lives. I can't count the number of times someone has come to me and said, "This church doesn't care. No one understands or makes any attempt to reach out to me. I'm not going to come anymore. This place is a poor representation of the body of Christ."

I used to nod and say, "I'm sorry to hear that" and go on with my day with a little chip on my shoulder. Now I begin to ask these people about their experiences and where they have felt misunderstood or abandoned. The list is sometimes long, but at the core is usually a recent experience of significant loss or trauma. What they really want to say is, "I hate God." They are enraged that he has allowed pain and heartache to invade their lives, and the church is an easier target for anger than God. You can see it. You can pound on its walls. You can yell at its people. You can stop coming. So there!

Usually, if these people have, in actuality, been well cared for and loved by the church, they will leave for six months to a year and then return. But sometimes people who project their bad

feelings onto churches will church-shop all their lives. They flit
here and there, never settling down to rest. As AA says, "Wherever you go, there you are." These people aren't running from
churches. They are running from themselves.

Churches can breed projection, especially when they emphasize that "we are righteous" and "they are sinful." If I am
"righteous," then all my problems can be attributed to society's
ills, to the riff raff who hang out by the corner liquor store, to
misguided laws, to bad people, to poor leadership, and to my
Aunt Betty who never shaves her legs.

Within the church community, spiritual rigidity and projection can reinforce defenses that inhibit rather than encourage
emotional healing. When we quote our words as God's words,
we use language as a lacquer to paint over deep-rooted problems. These problems will not go away unless they are dealt
with directly and genuinely. It would be a good discipline to
strip ourselves of Christian lingo and talk like the rest of the
world occasionally to see if there's any meaning under our re-
flexive sayings. "Praise the Lord" might be better received by
non-Christians (and me, too, actually) if we simply said, "Am I
ever grateful that I can live this day in God's presence." If this is
what you really mean, say it. Don't sugarcoat it or use religious
words to distance yourself from what's really going on inside—
good or bad.

Authenticity in speech and action from Christians would
come as a healing balm to many who stand outside the church,
perceiving it to be an irrelevant group of people who are per-

petually nice but generally ineffective when it comes to real life issues. Much of their attitude could be transformed if we would trust God and one another enough to lay on the line exactly what we think and feel. Good therapy can help us know what we think and feel if we are having trouble figuring it out. Then perhaps we can learn to use the words of Scripture effectively and with integrity, not as a means to perpetuate our defenses.

It has been a revelation to me that the more vulnerable I am in the pulpit—the more I get rid of spiritual pomposity and evangelical lingo and simply share my life experience including my foibles and failures—the more people resonate. When I express my brokenness, my uncertainty about what God is doing, or on the other hand my joy in the love of Jesus, people soak it up like dry sponges. They weep, they shake my hand, they want to talk more, they say, "Thank you!" All I have done is share honestly. It's that simple.

I am going to say it again: Stating the problem is the first step toward healing. In keeping ourselves honest and trusting God enough to be genuine before him and others, we can grow together as wounded but fellow travelers, all in need of God's love. The language of Jesus was always honest and nondefensive. It was meant to lift burdens, not lay them on heavier. The language of Jesus opened the way for us to enter the kingdom. It brought us freedom from isolation, from ourselves, from others and from God.

On the cross Jesus demonstrated ultimate vulnerability while revealing to us the utter despair of our own condition. When he appeared to the disciples as resurrected Lord, he wasn't ashamed of his wounds. He was resurrected with the scars still in his hands, and he showed them to his closest friends.

In Jesus' own body he joined pain, wounds, brokenness and the memory of horrific brutality with resurrection life and power. This is our story as Christians—in this world we live pain and resurrection together. Classically this has been called "the already and the not yet." The already is the resurrection joy of the Holy Spirit forming us, teaching us and alive in us. The not yet is the scars we bear, the brokenness and weakness in us, the areas where we are vulnerable and terribly human.

If hell on earth is being stabbed over and over with the same wound as we cycle through old patterns, heaven on earth must be the process of acknowledging our wounds as Jesus did, knowing where they are and not being afraid to show them to the world. The wounds of Jesus were the proof Thomas needed to believe in the resurrection.

If we are honest and genuine, we are not afraid to show our wounds. "To be alive is to be broken," states Brennan Manning in *The Ragamuffin Gospel*. We don't need a false spiritual language to coat over what is really going on. We don't need spiritual words to lacquer over the pain, scars and deep wounds that life inevitably brings. Rather, we can say, "Here, look! This should have killed me—this battle wound right here, and here and here. These are my scars. Take a good look at where I am imperfect and even downright disgusting. It is an amazing thing that I live, but I do! You can be just as amazed as I am at the goodness of God. Because Jesus lives and has set me free, so I live and am free. The very pain that ought to have destroyed me has actually made me stronger and more alive. And I don't blame you for these wounds. You are forgiven!"

⑥

What Happens When We Stop the Wheel

I met my husband, Tim, while I was attending Barnard College in Manhattan and he was at Columbia. As undergrads we dated for two-and-a-half years, and we got married two weeks after graduation. As I write this I have just celebrated my twenty-fifth wedding anniversary. But twelve years ago no one would have predicted that a twenty-fifth anniversary was on the horizon.

I had unwittingly married an alcoholic, and though I cared deeply for him, the same cycle of unpredictability, denial and false spiritual language that had marked my family of origin was now prevalent in our home. I was reliving my past and didn't know it. I was a "co"—codependent. I knew how to dance around and care for another person. I knew how to deny problems and convince myself things weren't so bad. I had done it for years with my mother, and I had never figured out that life could be different. I was wearing blinders, focused on how to survive rather than how to live. Meanwhile life was passing me by.

Being a "co" in our marriage worked for quite a while—thirteen years. Things weren't wonderful, but they were better than they had been when I was growing up. I kept holding on and making things work. Then my husband's alcoholism and prescription drug abuse skyrocketed as his productivity quotas increased at work. Life morphed into a nightmare. Tim lost his job. He became a man I didn't know. With a four-month-old, a two-year-old and a four-year-old I was desperate, once again at the receiving end of crazy and unpredictable behavior. One night I did what I had never done before. I opted out of the hamster wheel.

I woke up one morning and sensed the presence of God in a way I never had in the past. It was a directive presence with a sense of urgency about it. Perhaps Joseph experienced this same presence in his dream when the angel told him to take the infant Jesus to Egypt so he would be safe (Matthew 2:13-15). I knew very clearly that morning that the situation I was living in could not be healed by my resolve to stay in it. This clarity was a divine gift. The directive to leave was clear, firm and something I knew I must do quickly. A day later I took the three children, put them in the car and drove off. The next day I boarded a plane for California and went to visit a friend who had invited me to stay with her. "If you come out here," she told me, "I will help you. I will take care of you." And that's what I did.

Following God's directive did not mean the experience was easy. The next year and a half I was more lonely and exhausted than I could ever remember being. I longed for the man I loved, yet I knew I couldn't be with him. People told me to give up, to get on with my life—as if I had any clue how to do that. With three small children I could barely make it to the grocery store. I would put one child in the cart, strap another in a carrier and have the oldest run alongside. In an unfamiliar place with no family support, I felt like I was on an island, completely alone with no one but myself to depend on for my survival and my children's well-being.

Yet there was something different about this time of suffering than previous experiences. Things kept happening to me that assured me of God's presence. Prayers kept being answered. Hope seemed to invade my life for no reason. Like background music that creates a mood of drama, this assurance was a source of expectation, energy and life. People would look at me with disapproval—a single mom with three small kids! "A walking charity case," I heard someone whisper with a sidelong glance one day as I walked by. I felt like a complete loser, yet at the same time I had this deep unshakable assurance that somehow, in God's timing, all I had lost would be restored. I kept being pointed to a horizon where the sun was just about to come up. I was catching the early morning rays of hope. I was tasting it before there was anything to be hopeful about.

A year and a half later my husband, Tim, joined us. He had finally hit bottom and was in the beginning stages of recovery. Bit by bit, step by step, we worked our way back into each other's arms. Little by little trust grew between us as AA, counseling, prayer and people's love helped us along. We are now a family in recovery, and we will always be in recovery. In fact, it is our story of recovery that brings many to see Tim in his clinical psychology practice. They want someone "real," they say, who has been through it and come out on the other side. Tim and I have learned who we are, we have put first things first, we have hung on to one another for love's sake, and we have learned and continue to learn how to love. Our marriage is better than it has ever been, and as one that is refined in the furnace, so we have been changed.

Not that we don't still have our struggles, discouragements and differences. Our marriage is human, and it will never be perfect. But we have changed in such a way that we are not repeating old patterns of chaos and confusion. Getting off the hamster wheel was painful and difficult and exhausting—but so worth it! Both of us have gone to hell and back for the relationship that we are now able to enjoy. Someone once described us as Lazarus come back from the dead.

At times, Tim and I look at each other and just laugh. We weren't supposed to make it. We weren't supposed to hope. The odds were stacked against us. So we laugh because we see how good God is after everything has gone stale and life seems to have gone down the drain. In a cold, stone tomb resurrection happens. The sun does rise, the Lord is faithful, and people who get off the hamster wheel can be transformed.

During the days of our reconciliation, Tim and I realized that we couldn't simply build onto the precarious structure of our past relationship, adding another balcony to a toppling building with a poor foundation. What we had to do was dismantle and start over; knock down the old and build from the ground up, bit by bit, creating something healthy, secure and entirely new.

The knocking down part took place during our separation. The real challenge was the rebuilding—dismantling old patterns and finding new ways of relating. In order to do this we had to learn who we were as individuals first; only then could we come together as partners and lovers in a new way, committed and surrendered to God.

It was not easy. I emphasize this because many people believe that when you are in God's will, everything happens without pain. But Scripture says, "Beloved, do not be surprised at the fiery ordeal that is taking place among you to test you, as though something strange were happening to you" (1 Peter 4:12). For my husband and me, losing old habits and discovering new ways to listen and learn from each other took patience, persistence and prayer. The counseling we went through was brutal. I often wanted to give up. And yet the hard work, the pain and the ongoing challenge brought us somewhere. This kind of process is what I call potter's-wheel suffering.

The potter's wheel is different from the hamster wheel because it is redemptive. You get off it in a different shape than when you got on. It produces transformation. And yet the process of being molded is not necessarily pleasant. Potters slam the clay around a lot at the beginning. This hammering and pounding realigns molecules so that the clay can become stronger and hold up as the potter continues to work with it. If the clay could

talk, it would probably tell the potter that it didn't like being
slammed around one bit. But in that awkward lump the potter
sees the future result, and he continues to pound and mold
with hope and expectation. The clay does not move the wheel
at its own pace and for its own purposes the way the hamster
does. Rather, the potter drives the wheel as he sees fit. The clay
never finds itself alone on the wheel. The potter's hand is in the
mix and shapes the whole process, seeing the end from the beginning.

Potter's-wheel imagery is used both in the Old Testament
(Isaiah 29:16; 45:9; Jeremiah 18:6) and the New (Romans
9:21), always with God as the potter. This language is used to
emphasize not only God's sovereignty but his ability to right a
wrong and purify a wayward nation, even if it means pain.

> Does the clay say to the one who fashions it, "What are
>   you making"?
>   or "Your work has no handles"? (Isaiah 45:9)

My growth has meant pain. The potter's wheel has involved
a great deal of tears, prayer and psychotherapy, along with the
hard work of forgiveness and a deep resolve to endure so that
my shattered life could be "reset" and I could heal completely.

Before I got off the hamster wheel, I always felt a disconnect
when I read about Jesus coming to give us "abundant life" so
that "our joy might be made complete." I was supposed to be
living a certain way, but I couldn't seem to actualize it. I was
running around and around but not going anywhere. Not

changing. Not flourishing. Just surviving. I was working very hard—my brow was wet, my breathing heavy—but I always got off right where I got on. Isaiah puts it like this:

Why do you spend your money for that which is
  not bread,
    and your labor for that which does not satisfy?
Listen carefully to me, and eat what is good,
    and delight yourselves in rich food.
Incline your ear, and come to me;
    listen, so that you may live. (Isaiah 55:2-3)

Scripture is full of these claims, that though we live in a world full of agony and injustice, God's grace, mercy and compassion are more powerful than the deepest, darkest pit. When we do it God's way (which always involves the potter's wheel at some point), our souls come alive. We are not destroyed; rather we belong to the Author of Life and have a purpose and call that is larger than life. The abundant life is an awareness that I am caught up and involved in something bigger than myself, and this something is a Someone who is my liberator and friend.

"In him we live and move and have our being" (Acts 17:28). This brings a joy, a hope, a renewal that is larger than our circumstances. The presence of Jesus assures us that we are on the right wheel.

People can experience similar life circumstances and reach very different outcomes depending on what wheel they're on. Take the example of an extramarital affair, either sexual or emotional. I remember one woman who told me that she was left alone night after night while her husband talked on the phone with a female colleague whom he was trying to "help." The wife kept trying to get her husband's attention and lure him back. Her suffering and loneliness were profound, but they were of the hamster-wheel variety. This wasn't the first time the husband had become overly involved in helping attractive females. The pattern was not recognized, and no intervention was made —outside of the wife continuing to believe that she, on her own steam, could and would gain back her husband's love and attention. The couple did not seek marital therapy, and eventually the marriage disintegrated.

In a similar situation, a husband had an ongoing sexual affair but returned to his wife, deeply remorseful, after six months. The couple sought marital therapy and worked on the hard challenge of forgiveness. It was a painful process, but the result, years later, is a solid marriage and a happy family. Through the pain, this couple realized what mattered most. They got off the hamster wheel, got on the potter's wheel and ended up a different shape—a far better shape—than when they got on. Both situations were extremely painful, but the latter involved remorse, forgiveness, reaching out, getting help and a strong commitment to change on the part of both husband and wife.

Recently it occurred to me, after I had sat through several pastoral counseling sessions that were like a series of hamster wheels, one after the other, that when cyclical patterns become the norm, they form—if you will allow me another rodent-related metaphor—a maze with no exit. We might be on a path that looks like it's leading somewhere, but we find ourselves retracing our steps time after time. There is no way out unless we can somehow rise up from the maze vertically. Aha! An additional dimension is exactly what is needed. With it we can lift out of the maze entirely and be set down on a clean white expanse where we are no longer constrained by old patterns. We can actually go somewhere and experience new things! Realization of the need to move vertically happens once we admit that there is no horizontal exit.

In order to move vertically, we must be willing to reach out for another person's perspective. We have to realize that we're wearing ourselves out on a problem that has no solution from within the maze. For instance, if I had not left the chaos of my home and reached for outside help, I don't believe we would have recovered as a family. Had Tim not reached up from the maze of his addiction and sought help after he hit bottom, he would have destroyed himself. Had my mother been able to reach out and get professional guidance, our lives would have been far more healthy.

God's calling for each individual, which he longs to fulfill in us, can't be realized if we're following a pattern of futility. Old patterns do not bring change, though the temptation is to keep thinking they will. "The devil prowls around, looking for someone to devour" (1 Peter 5:8). "The thief comes only to steal and kill and destroy. I came that they may have life, and have it abundantly" (John 10:10). We are devoured when we run in circles. Our lives are stolen from us, and our hopes and dreams are killed off slowly over time. Old, tired patterns of futility will make us old and tired too.

Christ was all about breaking up old patterns. Do you remember to whom he first appeared after his resurrection? It was to women! In ancient times women were considered the worst witnesses. Their testimony wouldn't even hold up in court. Many women could not leave the house or courtyard without a man's permission. They were meant to stay passive and compliant, under the authority of father or husband. This was the old pattern—the norm. Yet Jesus taught something different. He taught women about trust and action. Trusting God, they were to move out in faith and become something new. They were to go and be his witnesses.

Moments before, the women had thought there was no way out of their predicament. Jesus was dead. His body was gone. Suddenly they turned around and everything they had thought was hopeless was gloriously full of life and wonder. The resurrection had put them in a new place and reshaped their perspective. The potter's wheel of the cross where they had wept led to a resurrection morning in which they were liberated. "You're it," Jesus declared. "You are my witnesses." It was up to them to respond.

Jesus asked the woman at the well to go and get her husband. He told the woman who was healed of the flow of blood to go in peace. He told the woman accused of adultery to go and sin no more. The word is *go*. Now that you have encountered me, he says, go and perpetrate life, not death. Jesus never issues a call to passivity—a mandate to retrace old patterns. He calls us to act on the reality that we are honored and loved. "Go in my name!" is a command that conveys tremendous worth. We go in the name of Jesus like ambassadors of a country or representatives of royalty. The call to pull ourselves out of old paths that foster oppression and fear and begin to represent the grace and mercy of Jesus is a call that sets us free.

Freedom from isolation, self-absorption and fear often comes from doing time on the potter's wheel. In *The Gifts of the Jews* Thomas Cahill writes that the Jewish people were the one ancient race that believed history was more than a cyclical process of life and death, endlessly repeating itself for no purpose— which was what the pagans believed at the time. The Jews believed that there was divine meaning in the flow of events and processes through time. They believed that God was involved and had a plan.

To find the plan God has for us, to see the significance of our existence, we must look at our lives honestly. In Henri Nouwen's classic *Can You Drink the Cup?* he tells his readers that before we drink the cup, we must hold it:

> Holding the cup of life means looking critically at what we are living. This requires great courage, because when we start looking, we might be terrified by what we see. Questions may arise that we don't know how to answer. Doubts may come up about things we thought we were sure

about. Fear may emerge from unexpected places. We are
tempted to say: "Let's just live life. All this thinking about
it only makes things harder." Still, we intuitively know
that without looking at life critically we lose our vision
and our direction. When we drink the cup without holding it first, we may simply get drunk and wander around
aimlessly. Holding the cup of life is a hard discipline. . . .
We need . . . to put both of our hands around the cup and
ask ourselves, "What am I given to drink? What is in my
cup? Is it safe to drink? Is it good for me? Will it bring me
health?"

Potter's-wheel formation is what Nouwen is talking about
when he says it is a hard discipline to hold the cup of life. The
familiar ways of doing things, even if they are unhealthy or destructive, feel safe if we don't look too closely. Moving from the
hamster's wheel to the potter's wheel can be scary. We might be
called to something unfamiliar and challenging. We know there
will be a period of formation and change. Looking critically at
our life reveals things we'd rather not see, and we can easily
avoid honest reflection with our current pace of life. I often
wonder if we keep the hamster wheel going at such a dizzying
speed not out of necessity but because we are unwilling to hold
our cup and look at who we have become. This frenetic cycling
keeps us off the potter's wheel and safe from the pain of formation. But it also keeps us in bondage and from being flexible in
God's hand.

I spoke at a recent women's retreat, and a potter actually molded a pot on a wheel next to me as I spoke about the importance of formation. And Sharon was no amateur. Her work had been featured in upscale magazines and her services contracted out by wealthy homeowners who wanted specialized pieces—in one case a whole wall of sculptured art.

However, despite Sharon's talent and creativity, standing on the platform that day was not easy for her. In molding a beautiful pot from an awkward piece of clay, she herself was taking a great risk. She had told me that she was very afraid to stand in front of people, and she was worried that the pot wouldn't come out right. I wanted to ask her some spontaneous questions about the process of working with clay, and she was concerned that she wouldn't have the right answers. She shared with me that she had spent the last two years caring for her critically ill daughter who had cancer. The care had been intense and grueling, and the daily grind had isolated and drained her. Her daughter was better now, but she herself was still recovering from the ordeal. She was far more comfortable doing pottery at home—not with large groups of people watching. In fact, she had never done this before. Working alone was more familiar and felt much safer.

"But I want to try," she said. "Despite all my nervousness, I want to reach out by sharing myself in this way. If the pot doesn't work out while you're talking, then I'll simply make another one. And if I don't know the answer to a question, I will just say 'I don't know.' This is a place where I need to grow. I need community and I want to go for it."

Here was a woman who was holding the cup of her life, examining it critically and making a conscious choice to move into an unfamiliar area so she could be shaped in a new way. It was scary; it was a challenge—but Sharon did it anyway.

It was a wonderful experience, both for me and for her. When we presented in front of the group, she answered my questions so easily that we let some people in the audience take the mike and ask questions as well.

Not only was Sharon providing a visual illustration of what I was talking about that evening, but the movement from hamster wheel to potter's wheel was happening in her own life in the context of a loving community of faith. The praise and affirmation from the group after she finished was profound. This woman, who had gone through so much alone, was surrounded by people who wanted to know her better. She recently mailed me a note along with a lopsided mug I had made at the retreat, which she had fired. In the note she said, "Anytime you do a sermon about the potter's wheel, I'll be happy to come and do it again."

You too can find a way out of the hamster wheel. It is different for each person, but there is always a way. When you fly on an airplane, the crew tells you to look around for the emergency-exit signs and become aware of the closest way out. They tell you that if you are sitting next to an exit and don't want to be in charge of opening it in an emergency, you should switch your seat with another passenger. Sometimes we don't know how to get out of a situation. We may need to look around, perhaps in a different direction, for a way out that we didn't know existed. Sometimes we know the way out but are too scared to open the hatch. We need someone else to help us through the exit process. When we're looking for a way out, it's important to remember that God loves to provide us with trap doors, passageways to freedom, unexpected rides "outta here." God is a master at leading his people out of bondage.

Scripture tells us that "no testing has overtaken you that is not common to everyone. God is faithful, and he will not let you be tested beyond your strength, but with the testing he will also provide the way out so that you may be able to endure it" (1 Corinthians 10:13).

A way of escape! God got the Hebrews out of Egypt in the book of Exodus. He got Daniel out of the lion's den without a scratch. God rescued Noah, David and Esther and her people. He rescued the prostitute from being stoned, the paralytic from immobilization, the widow who wept for her only son from overwhelming grief. God makes a way of escape that we might be able to bear it.

Often for people in the hamster wheel, clear paths of circumstantial escape are the first step to health and well-being. We may need to move out of an abusive relationship. We may need to stop perpetuating an addictive cycle. We may need to be more honest with ourselves, others and God about what is actually going on. We may need a weekend of retreat and prayer. We may need intensive therapy so we can work through trauma, loss or pain. We may need spiritual direction to help us find our call. We may need to change our priorities in the direction of love and service rather than frenetic activity and debilitating stress. We may need to seek out a friend or family member who will put us up for awhile. We may need someone to show us where the exit signs are in our lives.

Trying to be a better person is not a way of escape. It most often is a choice motivated by an unhealthy desire to "fix" a hamster-wheel situation, and it will go nowhere. It is like being chased by a monster in a dream. You can climb a tree, jump over the fence, even shoot the monster, but because it is a dream, he still keeps coming at you. Then you wake up! Being awake puts you in a completely different place, a danger-free zone with no monsters. Similarly, to leave the hamster wheel you must move into a completely different frame of reference, vertically out of the maze with no exit to a new place where you recognize God as liberator and intimate lover. This is the place where you can grow, learn and live freely without fear of attack.

One young woman I met with was a lawyer with two small children. She told me with tears that her husband, also very successful professionally, was a rage-aholic. He would corner her and yell in an outrage for long stretches of time, leaving her shaking and sick to her stomach. This had been going on for years, but recently it had escalated. Deeply committed to Christ, she kept praying for him and for guidance about what to do. In prayer one day, she invited Jesus to come into the scene in her mind where her husband had cornered her and was yelling. She saw Jesus quietly come alongside her and put his arm around her shoulders. Then he turned her away and together they walked out of the room together. A way of escape!

This woman's story got me thinking that we never escape the hamster wheel alone. We escape because God's arm is around us, leading us out of bondage and pain into safety, liberty and dependence on him. Just as the newly liberated Hebrew people had the pillar of fire and cloud with them in the desert, so in our desert of formation we can bear it because we are not alone.

Another example of a way of escape is illustrated by a couple with three children who had come to the United States from Australia. They had been separated for the better part of a year and divorce was imminent. The woman, who was living in Oregon, admitted to me that she had been critical and domineering as she tried to "lead her husband to the Lord." Separation, blow-ups and scattered fragmented relationships were chronic issues that she couldn't seem to resolve. One day in church, she had an experience of Jesus' love that told her she was supposed to move back to the area where her husband lived and just wait. After praying with others and talking with pastors and counselors, she jumped, in radical faith, completely out of the hamster wheel and moved herself and her children. In desperate faith she acted, even when it was very scary. Waiting was the worst of all. She knew she wasn't supposed to criticize her husband. She wasn't supposed to judge, manipulate or witness. She was just supposed to wait.

This was extremely difficult, especially when she discovered that her husband was living with another woman. She asked for prayer for strength and trust in God, even on days that seemed impossibly gloomy. Gradually, over time, as the couple shared childcare responsibilities and they saw more of each other, the husband realized that he still loved his wife. Together they committed to work on their issues, spend time together, communicate and grow. It wasn't easy for them to get on the potter's wheel and begin, but today they are reaping the fruit of their collaborative effort to get in step with their own transformation.

Once you have found your way of escape, several things will happen as you begin to grow and change. The next chapter identifies what will occur in the process of potter's-wheel formation.

(7)

Allowing God to Mold Us

My son is growing bean plants for a science experiment, and they are lined up on his desk by the window. The plants grow toward the light. They are stretching, reaching, extending their little shoots toward that window to get as much photosynthetic power as possible. Unfortunately, human beings do the opposite. The world says, "Stretch away from God! You don't need him—after all, you are a self-made individual. Reach toward what is fun, self-gratifying and of the moment. This will make you happy." (It doesn't mention that these things are often futile, empty and meaningless.)

Redirecting our lives can be painful, just like unclenching a fist hurts because the muscles have been constricted for so long. We aren't used to leaning toward God. We ache and stretch as we are pulled in a different direction. The result, however, of a posture inclined toward God is getting to know the self that was created for fellowship with him and to walk with God "in the cool of the day" (Genesis 3:8 NIV).

CHARACTERISTICS OF THE POTTER'S WHEEL

I have found in my experience as a pastor, as a teacher, and as a wife and mother that when God is at work to bring about transformation, suffering is somehow always involved. It is the nature of this fallen world that we must be broken, melted and reshaped by the potter in order to be like Jesus. It is painful because we are naturally inclined in the wrong direction. But how do we know if we are suffering because the potter is working on us or because we're trapped in a hamster wheel? I have provided some guidelines in this section to help us discern the difference.

- God's work is not cyclical; it is revolutionary. Change occurs. We get off the wheel in a different shape than when we got on.

- God's hand is involved in the process of formation. He is in charge and we are never alone, but it may get worse before it gets better.

- We may experience an awareness that we are being held and formed with loving intent. We may even get a glimpse of God's larger perspective regarding our call and purpose.

- The outcome brings new life for us and those around us. We have gone somewhere and become something new. Even if our circumstances remain unchanged, we have been liberated.

- We are not in a vacuum, nor are we in a "me and Jesus" endeavor. We have community—friends, pastors, counselors, therapists, lay ministers and prayer warriors to help us through.

With the help of our support systems and the encouragement of the Holy Spirit, we grow and deepen even though we have a hard time of it. Let's look at some of these ideas in more detail.

REVOLUTIONARY FORMATION

Think of a hamster running on his wheel. His focus is horizontal. He looks out through the wheel and sees his water bottle, the shavings and the bars of his cage. As he cycles, he can focus only on his little world, its props and its comforts.

Now think of the potter's wheel. It goes around too, but if you are the clay, lying on your back, where are you looking? Up. And this makes all the difference. This vertical focus "turns our eyes upon Jesus" as we experience difficulty. This is not just a warm sentimentality or a nice thought for superspiritual people who have visions of Christ up in the corner of the ceiling. This is for ordinary people who offer themselves as living sacrifices on the altar of God's grace. In AA language, it is called surrendering to a "higher power" and acknowledging that we are powerless over alcohol. Knowing that we cannot do what we need to for ourselves, we focus on the One who can.

I have shared with you how the suffering I experienced after I came to California was qualitatively different from the suffering I had been cycling through before. My focus was on God and what he could do rather than on the situation itself. In my case, I had to change where I lived to get focused in the right direction. Through this, revolutionary change took place for Tim and me.

As we grow dependent on God, we find paradoxically that we have more agency through the gift of the Holy Spirit. We are not trying to be something we are not. We do not need to move the wheel. We do not have to deplete ourselves. Another is doing it for us, and he does a far better job. We are being fashioned for the purpose of holding the mystery of God's Spirit alive in us. He not only forms us but then fills us and enables us to be and do what we couldn't be or do on our own steam. "'Not by might, nor by power, but by my spirit, says the LORD of hosts" (Zechariah 4:6).

As God's hand touches us, we remain flexible under his gentle, intentional pressure. As we are formed we look into the eyes of the potter and know that we are loved beyond belief. As an infant looks into the face of her mother and begins to recognize her, begins to smile, so we focus on the face of eternal love. Through relationship with Jesus, we are changed, revolutionized, transformed into living in "the glorious liberty of the children of God" (Romans 8:21 KJV).

IT GETS WORSE BEFORE IT GETS BETTER

The reality that our situation can deteriorate before it starts to regenerate can keep many people from completing—or even starting—the healing process. We all want to avoid pain; it's a natural inclination. That's why there are so many painkillers on the pharmacy shelves. But the absence of symptoms is much different than genuine healing. Healing the pain of the past involves a pain of its own. It involves reliving excruciating experiences, and this can be extremely difficult.

I am a strong advocate for therapy. I constantly refer people to therapists whom I trust and who have a strong personal faith of their own. I also recommend that survivors of abuse receive long-term therapy. Quick fixes for complex cases and severe trauma are like taking an Advil for a brain tumor. Life has taken its toll. It has taken a long time to get where you are. You need at least half as long to heal, and healing can be painful.

Therapy covers some rough terrain, especially if you have experienced a lot of grief or trauma. It is necessary to go back and excavate, to work through the trauma layer by layer with a safe person. A good therapist will know how much you can stand and will regulate the process accordingly so it doesn't destroy you. This gentle, consistent excavation paves the way for healing. Gradually space opens up inside you, and your head begins to clear. Old habits and norms are reworked into new ways of relating and of being in the world. Gradually you are freed to love, live and enjoy. The challenge is to hang on when the journey involves a good deal of emotional turmoil. Revisiting old feelings and dark moments helps you realize that, one, you are not alone, and two, you have not been destroyed by the pain. You are bigger than the trauma, more resilient than the pain, and your journey is bringing you out, not pulling you under. Eventually, the cobwebs clear and you begin to see through the clean, clear lenses of recovery and healing.

At this point, new options emerge. New energy becomes available as you stop working, either consciously or unconsciously, on the old patterns and start exploring wider horizons. This takes time, it takes tenacity, it takes a deep resolve to grow and heal despite the hurdles that must be overcome. In all this we must remember who God is—a companion on the way, a liberator, a healer, a restorer of souls, a rebuilder of ancient ruins and the maker of meaning and purpose in our lives.

Stepping out of the hamster wheel involves breaking an addictive cycle—and it can come with withdrawal symptoms similar to those associated with drug and alcohol addiction. We may need to "withdraw" from being people pleasers who enable. Or we may need to extract ourselves from frenetic activity, staying busy for busyness's sake. In doing either we may encounter a sense of emptiness that we must confront before we can heal. This is not easy. It is painful but well worth the journey. For many, the hamster wheel is simply too familiar to leave—better the hell you know than the abyss you don't. New ways of interacting with the world and with others are too scary to embrace. Lack of violence, predictability, healthy loving relationships, time for oneself, a purposeful and centered way of life may just be too threatening.

We have a pet bird, and her cage desperately needed to be cleaned one day. I didn't have time to do it at the moment so I let the bird out of the cage to experience the freedom of the back room. I thought it would be a relief for her to have more space and a cleaner environment for a little while. The phone rang just after I opened the door of the cage and, leaving the bird flying around the room, I went to answer it. When I returned, the bird was back in her dirty cage, sitting on her splintered swing. Freedom was unknown and scary. The dirt, the scuffed-up mirror and the poopy perch were all she had ever known. Like that bird, we often associate safety with what we already know, even if it is far less than what God wants to give us.

Jesus was always calling people to experience what they didn't know already. "Come follow me and I will make you fishers of people." "Be my witnesses." "Go ahead, Peter. Come to me walking on the water. When you slip up, I'll be there to catch you." The fact that Jesus is there makes dangerous undertakings feel perfectly safe.

GOD'S HAND IS IN THE THICK OF IT

The last thing I want to do is to create a formula that looks good on paper but has no lasting value in people's lives. So keep in mind that these distinctions provide a general way of thinking to be weighed with discernment and prayer as you move in the direction of emotional health.

Generally speaking, God's presence makes itself known as a "hopeful intruder" when circumstances have gone belly up. If we are on the right wheel, we will have an experience similar to that of Jesus—as he looked toward the cross, "an angel from heaven appeared to him and gave him strength" (Luke 22:43). It may take a while for this to happen, and the distinctions between the two wheels are not always neat and clean.

Clearly, in the mess of my childhood, grace invaded my life. I was in the hamster wheel with no way of physical escape, but I was assured that I was not alone. This was a form of spiritual escape for me even though I could not change my circumstances. I also think my experience of Jesus' love helped me get out of the hamster wheel when I was old enough. In this way, then, the potter's hand was on me even when I was in the hamster wheel. As Christ says in John's Gospel,

> What is born of the flesh is flesh, and what is born of the Spirit is spirit. Do not be astonished that I said to you, "You must be born from above." The wind blows where it chooses, and you hear the sound of it, but you do not know where it comes from or where it goes. So it is with everyone who is born of the Spirit. (John 3:6-8)

I can't tell you that if you are in the hamster wheel, God will never reveal himself to you. Sometimes he has to in order to get you out! I can't say either that if you are on the potter's wheel, God is going to be so real in every moment that you'll feel loving and superspiritual at every turn. No, Jesus suffered and felt as though God had forsaken him. But it ended in resurrection. There are no formulas, just general ways of thinking. So bear this in mind when I say that usually when you are being fashioned by God on the potter's wheel, you will feel sustained.

When you experience deep pain on the potter's wheel, this is good—it means you are not avoiding or denying but listening to yourself and to what is real. Even when hope seems like a distant relative, you have an awareness that you and God together are stronger than the pain, that it will not overcome you. Gradually, you begin to find confidence in yourself. Slowly but surely you notice yourself crawling out of the pit you've been in, perhaps with some mud on your face, but zealous to move forward and use what you have been through for good. The desire to use your wounds to heal others is a sure sign of potter's wheel formation. Paradoxically, the pain builds your confidence and sense of who you are in Christ—it doesn't snatch your dreams away. Rather dreams become possible to realize in an atmosphere of freedom and inner peace wrought from genuine healing.

THE PRESENCE OF COMMUNITY

Community is another key sign that you are on the right wheel. You will find that you are able to receive encouragement from people who care about you, who are all around you representing Christ. But this movement into community may be difficult. Survivors have been taught, usually from childhood, that they've got to do it on their own. It is a whole shift—a courageous move—to be able to say, "I can't do it on my own. I need help from God *and* I need help from the people of God." Reaching out to others arrests the hamster wheel and turns on the light so we can see our situation in a new way. But reaching out can be so difficult!

I am reminded of the story from homileticsonline.com of David, an eleven-year-old boy in the Midwest who was run over by a tractor. He was significantly injured and blinded, and he could move only his right arm. For months he lay immobile in the hospital. Doctors said that he should have been getting better, but his refusal to respond to their efforts hinted at disillusionment in his spirit. He didn't want to try. His mother sat and kept vigil with him. In the bed next to her son was a year-old baby boy who would not stop whining. He was agitated and upset, and nothing seemed to calm him down. One day, in desperation, David's mother picked up the fussy baby and placed the child right on her son's chest. At first David didn't respond. The baby fussed and moved uncomfortably. Then, slowly, David began to move his good arm. He lifted it for the first time since the accident and gently began to stroke the little boy's back. It was the beginning of his recovery, and a relationship developed between David and the infant that nurtured and healed them both.

Sometimes we've been so lambasted, crushed and bruised by life that we just don't care anymore. We can't try. We feel as though we can't change anything for the better, and we don't care that we can't. We become immobilized by the overwhelming flood of difficulty that we have experienced. So any effort to reach out, even a feeble one, can require tremendous energy. It can even signify desperation.

If someone reaches out to me, I assume as a rule that this may be their one and only attempt to get the help they need. The person may be drowning, and this may be their last chance to show me that they're going down. I swoop in with life rafts of supportive networks and helpful people. I sometimes overdo it, I know, and people kindly tell me that they just wanted to know when the grief and loss support group met, or how they could get a lay minister to visit a few times. I overreact because I know how difficult it can be for survivors to reach out. This may be the last time they act on the dim and fading hope that things can be different.

If someone comes to you for help, don't ever underestimate how hard it may have been for them, and respond with all the love you can muster. If you are the one who doesn't want to try anymore, my prayer is that you will reach out one more time— or make an attempt for the first time. It can mean the difference between life and death. It can move you from hamster wheel to potter's wheel. Once you let others into your pain, they testify to the fact that not only is the potter forming you, he is also forming them and forming the church.

It is within this community of Jesus Christ that healing occurs. The church was called together at Pentecost as a human representation of the body of Christ. Therefore each of us must become acquainted with our own brokenness and walk alongside others who are also broken. This is what Jesus did. As we walk through suffering with one another, we remember that our true home is not here but in heaven where we will have perfect fellowship with God.

The mission and purpose of the Christian community is to be Christ to one another, walking in the way of the cross, bearing one another's burdens, invoking God's presence for healing and wholeness, yet always pointing to the ultimate victory that is ours as we move homeward to resurrection and perfect fellowship with our Creator.

VERTICAL FOCUS

Another sign that you are on the right wheel is that your gaze is vertical rather than horizontal. The circumstances surrounding you are important but do not determine your state of mind. Joy may come to you for no apparent reason. Your awareness of God shifts your priorities toward service, love, people and enjoying the moment. There is a willingness to surrender on the potter's wheel that is not apparent in the hamster wheel. There is a peace that is not passive but courageous—it is the courage to change the things we can and the discernment to know what we can't.

To change what we can, we might need to take drastic measures to make ourselves safe and begin again with new people in new ways. We might need to try out-of-the-box possibilities that we didn't have the courage to try before, or that we didn't even see. We might need to decide that what we thought was so important for so long, what we had been giving our lives to, isn't actually important after all. Pushing the "reset" button on priorities, living out of the divine center of grace and love, and knowing our purpose and call are all fruits of the potter's wheel. Suffering on the potter's wheel produces character (Romans 5:3-4).

NEW LIFE WITHOUT CIRCUMSTANTIAL ESCAPE

For you, there may be no possibility of escaping from your circumstances. Perhaps you are the caregiver for an alcoholic family member who is chronically ill as a result of his addiction. Perhaps you are a single parent struggling to make ends meet as you wait for checks from a former spouse who refuses to work. Difficulty presents itself in countless ways, and life marches on. Sometimes it's all you can do to live one day at a time.

I speak from my own experience. There was no way out for me growing up. One day when I was about twelve years old, I had been told too many times that I was evil, that I was not good enough for anyone to speak to and that my attitude was sending me to hell. In desperation I downed a fistful of aspirin and lay on the couch waiting to die. I couldn't even do that right. Nothing happened, and when I tearfully told my parents what I had done, they were outraged. I was ungrateful and rebellious—far more a loser than I had been before. I couldn't win. No one suggested that I needed counseling, or group therapy, or even a consistent youth group to attend. No one wanted to admit that there was a problem that was not me. The way out was barred, locked, shut. It appeared hopeless—until Jesus came in with his love. That was my escape from finite despair into infinite grace. I still suffered. I still went into depression in the hamster wheel. But I had something to hold on to after that experience—Jesus' presence in the midst of it. This kept me sane and alive.

In these instances, the way of escape may not be circumstantial. It may be spiritual. Peter was released from prison by the angel. He was free to go wherever he wished! Paul was imprisoned and actually awaiting execution as he wrote to the Philippians. Yet the way he wrote, you would hardly know it. He was full of the Holy Spirit, not oppressed or ground down by his circumstances. Philippians is the most joyful letter in the New Testament. Escape routes are sometimes circumstantial, sometimes spiritual, but they always move us toward freedom and purpose.

I knew a woman who had a son, Kyle, who suffered with severe cerebral palsy. Her suffering was not brought about by any sinful behavior, but it was still very difficult for her to cope. She could have found herself on a hamster wheel of overresponsibility and anger as she cared for her son. Yet in the midst of the pain, as she and others prayed, she and her family began to change. Gradually Kyle became a gift rather than a problem. The love he showed them, the way they learned about dependence on God through Kyle's dependence on them, the way they drew people into their lives and gave to so many—these were all testimonies of the potter's involvement in this family's pain. Redemption, healing and love told me that God was working. The focus was always more on God than on circumstances, their outlook was hopeful, and each moment with Kyle was precious.

I do not think God ordained Kyle to be sick. I believe that, ultimately, God wants everyone to be well, whole and complete. I do think, however, that the channels of God's grace overcame suffering to create greater love, joy and right priorities in that family than if Kyle had not been born. Here there was no circumstantial means of escape. The family could have taken the advice of doctors and institutionalized their son, and yet for them (not for everyone), the right choice was to care for him. As they did they grew closer, fell more in love and relished the opportunity to share the faithfulness of Jesus with other families who had disabled kids. This is potter's-wheel formation.

Here are some questions you can ask yourself when you are in a situation that provides no circumstantial escape:

- Where can I go to get ongoing, consistent prayer?

- How can I get support from others who are going through a similar experience?

- Where can I find a safe place to be authentic and share, without "lingo," what is really going on inside of me?

- What possibilities exist for ministry—for serving others— out of my difficult experience? (Sometimes we need time, space and healing before we can even think about this. The last thing we want to do is serve others out of our own need to be served. But sometimes taking action like this promotes the healing process.)

- How can I discover new venues of expression and opportunity that will bring me joy and fulfillment? What will keep me from losing myself in this experience?

Do you see how these questions can move you out of the hamster wheel? Looking for the answers will shift you from isolation into community, from perilous places into safe places where you can be authentic. These questions encourage you to seek joy and opportunity and to move forward in relationship with God and others. These questions foster a sense of identity that is resilient, creative and liberating.

I must say a word about safe places. Unfortunately, churches don't always qualify. One couple I know shared with their pastor that their son, who had been a missionary, had suffered a mental breakdown. The pastor responded that this had happened because of sin in their son's life, then he shooed them out of his office and never called them again. You can imagine that this couple became estranged from that church. For this pastor, a simplistic answer to a complex problem was all he could offer. He was threatened by the misery of the situation and decided that rather than deal with the pain of it, he would dismiss it from his mind.

It took this couple a while to find a safe church that addressed mental illness both from a sound spiritual perspective and a sound psychological one. Out of their hurt, confusion and longing for fellowship, they founded our church's HELP group for healing, encouragement, love and prayer. Be careful, discerning and prayerful before sharing with anyone. A good rule to remember is that Jesus is a lifter of burdens. He never lays on a bent back another weight. "A bruised reed he will not break" (Isaiah 42:3; Matthew 12:20).

NEVER IN ISOLATION

The importance of community, of being "all together in one place" (Acts 2:1), goes back to the disciples' emphasis on gath-

ering together when the early church was formed. The very fact
that God created the church reveals that he didn't mean for us
to go it alone. We were meant to "bear one another's burdens,
and in this way you will fulfill the law of Christ" (Galatians 6:2).
That's a pretty incredible law, if you ask me—holding one another up, keeping each other in prayer, doing "small things for
one another with great love," as Mother Teresa said.

The movie *Awakenings* with Robert De Niro depicts people in
a psychiatric ward who are completely immobilized. No one be-
lieves that these patients have any mental ability until a doctor
played by Robin Williams begins administering a drug that
wakes them up. Suddenly they can move, they can talk, they can
interact with their families. Their old personalities return. Heart-
breakingly, the drug's effects wear off, and the people eventually
return to their inert state. This story is based on the true account
of Oliver Sacks, who wrote about it in a book called *The Man Who
Mistook His Wife for a Hat*. While the movie portrayed all of the
patients returning to immobility, Sacks reports that in fact most
of the people with one significant person in their life stayed
awake and did not regress. This speaks strongly for the power of
relationship, love and human contact. Our identity, our meaning
and our desire to live comes out of meaningful relationships.

The church I am involved in tries to provide concrete ways
for people to reach out and find help. We provide many recovery and support groups—quite a smorgasbord, in fact. This is
because we believe transformation happens in small groups
that provide healing, prayer and a safe haven. We believe that

God works through this network of support systems, all of which are staffed by laypeople who simply feel called to give back in the name of Jesus.

It has been shown that many people come to church for the first time simply because another person invites them. Sometimes all we need is one person who cares. Maybe you can be that person for someone else. Or maybe you can reach out to the one person who will be the difference between life and death for you.

8

Discovering Potter's-Wheel
Formation Through Prayer

Jeffrey, a junior-higher involved in our church youth program, is an expert swimmer. He has broken records of all kinds, and he amazes those who watch him. People stand in awe and shake their heads as he swims—not just because of his speed and competency, but because this young man has a debilitating, progressive lung disease that may eventually prove fatal. In a sport that requires rhythm in breathing and good lung capacity, his excellence in swimming baffles. Many people are praying for Jeffrey's complete and total healing, and his parents are in a small group that provides support for the family. Discouragement, however, can set in. One day Jeffrey turned to his Mom and asked, "Mom, why doesn't God just do a miracle?"

Without missing a beat, his mother turned to him and replied, "Honey, *you* are the miracle."

Suffering. It may not be alleviated. There may be no way to

escape the pain of our circumstances. But through intentional prayer, miracles happen in the midst of our pain that remind us of the potter's presence and power.

I am aware that in writing about suffering, I am walking a tightrope. I want to adequately address all the foibles and pitfalls of our human condition that keep us in bondage to things that are not God's will. However, I do not want to overpsychologize and underspiritualize. There is no doubt that God is able to do "abundantly far more than all we can ask or imagine" (Ephesians 3:20). No matter where we are, no matter how badly we have messed up, no matter what our story, our pain, our grief—there is a Redeemer. There is always hope because there is always Jesus. And hope comes about in different ways for different people. None of us know the outcome of our own story. Miracles happen, even when they are different from what we expected.

The power of prayer is real. I oversee a healing service at our church—a simple service with only thirty or so people who attend. We have Communion and then we pray individually for those who request it. There is no hype, no calling people to the front to "testify," no long-winded expositions; it is simply a brief meditation, Communion and prayer. This important gathering is one of the few times in a large church when people can spontaneously receive one-on-one care. I feel privileged that people allow me into their story, into their pain, and grant me the honor of praying for them. I can't believe I get paid to do it.

In this service people are regularly healed. Many wonderful

things happen very quietly. One person who needed jaw surgery received prayer and her jaw was realigned. She didn't need the upcoming operation. A woman who loved to hike had to stop because of back pain. As she was prayed for, her back stopped hurting. Now she hikes all over the place. Someone else asked for prayer for a son who had been hospitalized for several days with a serious internal rash. We prayed, and the next day the rash was gone. I took a member of our healing team with me to pray for a woman who was in a coma. As we laid hands on her the Holy Spirit's presence was palpable. In two days she was back home. I could go on.

People are also healed of their emotional pain. One person had grown up with severe abuse. It was ritualistic, and it took every form I had ever heard of. I was horrified as I listened to this individual share the awful abuse that had been present during childhood—every day, year after year. This person regularly attended the healing service, which was quieter, with fewer people, than the larger service and provided a greater feeling of safety. Communion was meaningful—one-on-one prayer essential.

Over the years that this person has been coming, healing has happened. Growth has occurred. It is not just the healing service that has helped. It is counseling, it is the men's fellowship, it is friends, it is this person's hard work to stay on track and be faithful in asking for help. This person now has a joyful demeanor, a centeredness that has replaced nervous agitation, and a light in the eyes. I am amazed that this individual has had the courage to keep coming, keep pursuing health and whole-ness, keep moving forward.

If ever I forget, this service reminds me of the power of prayer and of Jesus' longing to make us whole and complete. In a lot of this stuff, we don't wrestle against flesh and blood. We have an Enemy and we can't get through life victoriously unless we know how to pray deeply and regularly. There is no substi-tute for prayer. If Jesus needed it, we certainly do as well. We may not understand everything we are up against in the spiri-tual realms, but we do know that Jesus is big enough and alive enough to take it all on for us. Getting to know him ought to be the extreme focus of our prayer life.

Although God can do anything, he asks for our cooperation and participation. He wants our input, our love, our invest-ment. No prayer goes unheard by God, but the way we pray can shut him out rather than invite him in. There is a divine cour-tesy about Jesus. He is not pushy. An invitation must be given. There must be a place set aside so he can come in and sit down. The latch must be opened, the door swung wide. There must be a willingness on our part to encounter the Someone we have been "talking at" all our lives but may never have experienced with any intensity. This can be scary.

When I have company over that I don't know very well, I al-ways feel a little awkward, harboring a slight fear that I will be disapproved of. Will my guests notice the stains on the carpet? Will they dislike my cooking? Will the conversation be easy, or will it be stilted and forced? Still, I go through with it, and each time I have those same people over, it gets easier and easier. I don't have to start from scratch. I already know them. I am developing a relationship.

I have found out that making space for Jesus is nothing less than making space for the best company you will ever have. There is no judgment, no disapproval, no raised eyebrow at the stains of my life. Rather, there is great appreciation for my invitation, and the conversation is always full of grace. There is centeredness and the feeling that Julian of Norwich expressed when she wrote, "All shall be well, and all shall be well, and all manner of things shall be well." Feeling this way unknots my need to control. I can surrender and thereby have time to really love—to love Jesus, to love my family, to love myself, to love others.

In order to make space for transformation in our lives, we may need to change the way we pray. I sure did. I realized at one point that I was doing a whole lot of talking and not much listening. I had always been "in charge," thinking I had to hold everything together through prayer. Realizing that I was not the one who made things happen in my prayer life was a huge hurdle that I had to overcome. And surrender does not come easily to me. As I have said again and again, changing old patterns is difficult. Trying something new feels awkward at first. Gradually, however, familiarity grows and the new way becomes less difficult, and then enjoyable.

When God asks Jeremiah to go down to the potter's house, Jeremiah observes that the pot being created is flawed. The result? The potter "reworked it into another vessel, as seemed good to him" (Jeremiah 18:4). The clay at this point is still malleable enough to be reshaped. In the next chapter, however, Jeremiah buys a pot that has already hardened (Jeremiah 19). It cannot be reformed. Jeremiah throws the pot down and it breaks into pieces, illustrating the impending destruction of Judah and Jerusalem. The hardened vessel cannot be used for God's purpose, so it is destroyed.

Prayer is what keeps us moist in God's hands—pliable, flexible, moldable, usable. The rigid old patterns that would destroy us soften as we open ourselves to the presence of Jesus and make space for him in our lives, allowing him to take over. Here are some suggestions for prayer that can open us up to potter's-wheel transformation.

MOVING FROM SOLILOQUY TO SILENCE

Rarely in prayer or Bible study groups does silence takes precedence over words. It is easy for us to wax eloquent and demonstrate great spiritual verbosity, never stopping to hear what God might be saying back to us. Being silent before God is a hard discipline to pull off. People tell me that they can't do it. It's too hard. Their mind wanders, they think about taking the dog to the vet or how much mayonnaise to put in the chicken salad. "I'm not wired for this," they say. "It's just not me."

While silence is certainly easier for some than for others, it is a discipline that can be learned by anyone. Eugene Peterson calls it a "disciplined, intentional passivity."

Spending time alone with God is not meant to draw us back into isolation. While there may be times when we are called to "go to a deserted place" like Jesus did, the result is for us to be strengthened so we can go back into the world loving the way Jesus did—sacrificially and meaningfully. Henri Nouwen in *Making All Things New* puts it this way:

> Without solitude it is virtually impossible to live a spiritual life. Solitude begins with a time and a place for God and him alone. If we really believe not only that God exists but also that he is actively present in our lives—healing, teaching and guiding—we need to set aside a time and a space to give him our undivided attention.

Our silence in God's presence is a space that we give him so that our agenda can be replaced by his agenda. Hamster-wheel prayers are noisy and may sound something like this: "Lord, I just thank you that I can come before you today and bring this list of requests to you. Please help so and so, and so and so, and also help me get everything done today to get ready for my housewarming party. I pray that you would get my son off of his duff and make him find a job. Be with everyone and bless them. Amen."

If we pray this kind of prayer, God certainly listens. He always listens. But sometimes we don't let God get a word in edgewise. It's all about us and what we think is important that day. Or we cycle through rote prayers, barely giving our words a thought since we have said them so often. I recently learned that until a few hundred years before Christ, it was against Jewish law to write out a prayer—any prayer that did not emanate from the heart was considered blasphemous. The apostle Paul tells us clearly that "we don't know how to pray as we ought" (Romans 8:26). Prayers that are effective and liberating are those that allow the Holy Spirit to pray through us. God's words become our words. His thoughts our thoughts. This happens slowly as we grow into learning how to listen and then receive God's agenda.

If the person praying the prayer above would take time to listen, she might begin to feel more love for her son, and perhaps a thought would come to her about how to interact with him in a helpful way rather than an angry way. Listening might help her to slow down and realize she has already done all that's necessary for the party. Jesus told Martha, "There is need of only one thing," to sit at his feet (a place usually reserved for men— at the feet of the rabbi) and listen (Luke 10:38-42).

When we stop and listen, we often experience a shift in perspective. What seemed so important moments ago fades into the background. Other things such as Jesus' love and the people in our lives come into the foreground.

Here's another hamster-wheel prayer: "Lord, please make me a better person. I'm supposed to do what my husband wants, but I'm sick and he doesn't believe me. I had a fever and he made me prepare dinner. When I went to lie down he pulled the covers out from under me and I fell on the floor. I must be doing something awful to make him so angry. Help me be a better person. Amen."

This is the prayer of someone who is running in the wheel of abuse. It is the wrong prayer, even though it is a cry for help. Answered prayer in this case—becoming a better person—will provide no relief for the victim. Something will always be "wrong" with her. The abuse will continue and will escalate until she has the courage to leave. A prayer that might open her to change could be, "Lord, give me your thoughts and your Holy Spirit. Help me to see your perspective and your will in this situation. Lord have mercy on me. I open myself up to your care for me."

It is not that God doesn't hear the first prayer or won't help this person. If God didn't respond to flawed and misguided prayers, we'd all be in trouble. But an open-ended prayer in which we invite God's initiative is the way we find true refreshment. We don't find relief in controlling every minute we spend in God's presence. Rather than asking God to come up with the answers to our dilemma and telling him what the solution should be, it is better to ask him what he has for us and invite him to act accordingly.

I used to always pray at the end of my counseling sessions in a rote way that indicated we were done and it was time to go. It was a kind of escort out the door. I am getting to the point now where instead of plunging in with words that fill the air, I ask if it would be OK to spend a few moments in silence listening, inviting Jesus to come be with us. Then if words come, they come. If not, they don't. True prayer is inviting Jesus in, letting his words become our words, his thoughts our thoughts. By creating space in this way, the Spirit has the freedom to come intercede for us with "groans that words cannot express" (Romans 8:26). There is a depth of prayer that words cannot plumb. Remember the verses from Isaiah?

> Why do you spend your money for that which is
>   not bread,
>   and your labor for that which does not satisfy?
> Listen carefully to me, and eat what is good,
>   and delight yourselves in rich food.
> Incline your ear, and come to me;
>   listen, so that you may live. (Isaiah 55:2-3)

What gets us out of futility and circular effort? Listening for God's voice. Giving ear to what God has to say to us about our life and our call. Hearing God's song of love in our heart makes our soul live. As Julian of Norwich states,

> We are so preciously loved by God that we cannot even comprehend it. No created being can ever know how much and how sweetly and tenderly God loves them. . . . Therefore we may ask from our Lover to have all of him that we desire. For it is our nature to long for him, and it is his nature to long for us.

When two people are in love, they can't wait to converse. They can't wait to hear what the other has been doing all day; they want to know each other's hopes and dreams, thoughts and desires. If we are in love with God, we will want to hear his voice—we will long for it. The more we love God, the more we will want to grow quiet so we can hear him. It may take a while to catch on. Just as Samuel heard God call his name but didn't know it was God, we might have a few false starts. Our world is noisy with many distractions, and the most harmful distraction is the inclination to feel guilty about not doing our prayers "right." When you experience these disturbances, gently bring yourself back to listening; if your mind wanders or you fall asleep, so be it. The disciples themselves couldn't stay awake when Jesus was with them in the flesh!

Jan Johnson recently wrote an article on prayer for *Conversations*, a journal about spiritual formation. She refers to different voices in the mind as committee members whose distracting messages play into our own unhealthy dynamics, causing us to feel guilty, overextend ourselves, feel superior about helping others, and so on. It is important to recognize these voices, name them, and then lay them aside, refocusing on what God is actually saying. Doing this helps us set aside negative associations with scriptural meditation and find freedom and relationship as we move toward interacting fully with the very life of God.

It is important to keep trying! Setting aside fifteen minutes a day to be quiet in God's presence can lead to transformation and tremendous spiritual growth. It can also help us hear in our souls what God is doing when we find ourselves on the potter's wheel. Following are some exercises that have been helpful for people as they began to change the way they prayed. Doing these kinds of prayers regularly will move you from closed, controlled soliloquy to an open-ended, receptive posture.

PRAYING THE SCRIPTURE

For people whose minds wander (which is just about everyone) or who are depressed and have a hard time concentrating, praying the Scripture can help. Try the following exercise: Choose a verse or short passage that is particularly meaningful for you. For the sake of illustration, let's use the verse, "There is therefore now no condemnation for those who are in Christ Jesus" (Romans 8:1). Say each word slowly and carefully. Ask the Holy Spirit to come and reveal the meaning these words have for you today, right now. Say them again, prayerfully, aware that God's presence surrounds you and that these are his utterances to you in love. Breathe deeply and let the words of the text fill you up inside. What would it mean if you really believed this—that there was no condemnation in Christ Jesus? How would you feel? How would you live? Close your eyes and open your palms in your lap. Pray the words, saying them again, realizing that they are true because they are God's words, and God does not lie. Allow the Holy Spirit to take you on from there, saying the words as often as you need or simply resting in God's love. If you journal, write down any insights that came to you during this time. If you do this with other people, share together after you are done.

This is a different way of reading Scripture than dissecting it—chopping it up to find everything we can about its historical content and garnering all the data possible. In a *Conversations* article Brian McLaren likens it to the two ways we can know a frog. We can dissect a frog and lay it open, learning all its parts as it lies there dead and cold. Or we can observe that frog living and active in its natural habitat, jumping from lily pad to bank to log. The latter is like praying the Scripture. It is a way to let the living words of God do what they do best as with disciplined passivity we let Scripture "read" us and allow it to bring about change.

GUIDED PRAYER

Sometimes guided prayer helps people create space in which to hear God's voice and receive his guidance. The following is an exercise in praying the Lord's Prayer (Matthew 6:9-13). Creating this kind of meditative prayerful attitude allows the Holy Spirit to at least slow down the hamster wheel for a time. Think about each part of the passage as you pray.

Our Father. This is a gracious address. Jesus doesn't keep his intimate relationship with God for himself but includes us all in it. Rest for a moment in the reality that Jesus' closeness with God is also something you are invited to participate in.

In heaven, hallowed be your name. God is other than us. Dwell in the assurance that Christ is the bridge from our brokenness to God's bright and beautiful reality.

Your kingdom come, your will be done, on earth as it is in heaven. Ask God for a few moments to make what's "up there" in heaven come "down here" in your life. Then ask him to create

in you a longing for his kingdom to be established on earth—
at your workplace, in your family, with your friends. Pause and
think about what this would look like for you.

Give us this day our daily bread. This is a call to trust. Relax for
a moment in the truth that each day God will be enough for you
and will provide for you. That's what he promised. Allow yourself the comfort of trusting him.

And forgive us our debts, as we also have forgiven our debtors.
This is the only statement with a condition. Ask Jesus to help
you love the world enough to let go of any grudges or resent-
ments you have been holding. Ask him to forgive you for anything you need it for, and receive that forgiveness completely.

*And do not bring us to the time of trial, but rescue us from the evil
one.* Fear is the enemy of the saints. Absorb the reality of the
good shepherd leading you in safe places—keeping you, holding you, protecting you.

When you are ready, open your eyes and reflect on any insights you received.

CENTERING PRAYER

I learned about centering prayer (even though I didn't know
then what it was called) when we were attacked by a mother
bear high above the timber line in the Adirondacks of New
York. We were in our Sears pop-up tent, which was basically
made of Saran Wrap. The baby bear had wandered into our
campsite a few moments earlier and had been scared off by a
backpack falling to the ground off a tree branch. When the

mother came racing into our campsite, there was no ignoring her. She threw logs, ripped open zippers, tore backpacks, scattered dishware. Tim did what he had learned in the camping guide we had purchased at the ranger station—bang pots and pans together to scare off the bear. Guess what? It didn't work. She came charging at the tent, pushing her big flat head against the Saran Wrap wall that threatened to cave in on us, and she roared with horrible halitosis just inches from my face.

I was not feeling particularly spiritual at the moment. I could not pray. I was shaking like a leaf lying there in my sleeping bag. Tim was scared too. After all, he was the one who had banged all those pots together! We waited with lumps the size of golf balls in our throats and heard our hearts pounding out what we thought to be the very last beats of our lives. But then these words came to my lips: "Lord Jesus Christ, have mercy on me." As I whispered them a peace flooded me that was from a Source outside myself. As the furious bear circled the tent I became calm. Finally, as I continued to whisper these words, she crashed off into the bushes and left.

Centering prayer helps at moments like these. Learning some simple phrases such as "Lord Jesus Christ, have mercy on me" or "Come, Lord Jesus" or "Be with me, O Lord; hold me in your steadfast love" can help us in times of crisis when we don't have a clue where to begin. When these words become internalized, the Holy Spirit prays them for you at moments when you cannot.

These phrases can be used also in our regular times of prayer.

Breathing deeply, in and out, we can imagine ourselves breathing in the Holy Spirit and exhaling any tension or anxiety. We can ask for forgiveness, and then we can imagine ourselves opening our hands and releasing any resentment we are holding. As we do this we can pray our phrase again and again, perhaps visualizing a cross or another symbol of God's love. As we repeat the words over and over, cultivating an attitude of love and openness, we stay in a posture of receptivity and create space for Jesus to flood us with his presence.

Prayer is a conduit for the work of the Holy Spirit. It opens a channel through which we make ourselves available to God's healing touch. Whenever we surrender in prayer as has been described, even if we don't realize it, we have been shaped in some way by the Potter's hand.

9

Finding Ourselves in a New Place

All that I have said up to this point is for one purpose only—to free the people of God so they can live triumphantly as the church Jesus died to save. That is why I have shared my own story so openly—that it might prove redemptive for you. If a traumatic event has occurred in your life, whether a recent incident in an ongoing cycle or something that's happened for the first time, it doesn't have to keep you in bondage. Here is a summary of the process of transition from hamster wheel to potter's wheel.

1. *State the problem.* It is common to deny the significance of trauma, to minimize the issue and therefore not take steps to get help. So the first step is to admit there is a problem. Be sure that superficial spiritual language is not masking the pervasive underlying issues that need to be articulated and addressed. If the problem involves violence, depression or other mental illness, addiction, depletion or an ongoing repetitive pattern,

chances are talking about it within your family system won't do the trick. Under these conditions, even if you can articulate the problem, you will need some kind of outside assistance to help you work it through. No one can put out a fire from inside the building that is collapsing on them.

2. *Reach out.* Maybe you don't know what the problem is, but you know you are being dragged down and feel hopeless most of the time. In order to articulate the correct problem, you may need outside expertise to discover the issue. Summon up your courage and reach out for help. Be sure it is safe help.

3. *Begin to seek God in some of the "open-ended" ways we talked about in chapter eight on prayer.* For further learning in this area, I recommend Dallas Willard's book *The Spirit of the Disciplines.* Also, be sure to get ongoing prayer support from people who know how to pray. Form a prayer chain or find one where people can receive prayer every day on a consistent basis. In our prayer-chain ministry, the person being prayed for will "check in" biweekly, which helps the pray-ers know what is happening, how to pray and when to rejoice.

4. *Involve others in your journey.* As I have emphasized repeatedly, our wounds are not meant to stay hidden forever. We may not want to just spill our guts anywhere or to just anyone, and this is appropriate. Good boundaries are necessary. At the same time, as you grow and heal, involving others in your journey toward health and wholeness will make you realize that you are not alone. As you open up, you indirectly give others permission to open up as well.

5. *Look for opportunities.* As you begin to feel stronger, ask yourself where God is calling you to serve. Where can your wounds be used redemptively? How can you bring freedom and healing to others? As you explore possibilities, it may well be that your healing will be enhanced through giving. A cautionary note: The timing here is very important. The last thing you want to do is to give before you have learned to receive or to give in order to avoid the pain of potter's-wheel transformation. Be sure to share your ideas for service with people who have walked with you through your pain to see what they say and to ask for prayer support.

There is nothing easy about working your way from hamster wheel to potter's wheel. It was difficult for my husband and me to get help and get healed—we didn't change wheels in a flying leap. Little by little we dealt with our problems, addressing them gradually in therapy and making a conscious effort to change old patterns.

Tim and I went out to dinner recently and had a marvelous time at our favorite restaurant. Out of the blue, he turned and looked at me.

"Thanks so much for taking me back into your life," he said.

"I love you," I replied.

"It wasn't easy," he said, looking at me with steady hazel eyes. "It was a tremendous risk."

"That's what you do when you love someone. You risk. You are worth taking back."

Then I cried. I cried because it had all worked out so darn

well, despite all the doomsday predictions and heartache. We had gone somewhere together! It had been a potter's-wheel process.

I sat not long ago with a man from another church who had given his life to the ministry and whose wife had been unfaithful. It had been a terrible ordeal. The couple was well known, and the scandal had rocked the congregation and the community in many ways. This man was going through a period of seeking the Lord and trying to figure out how to get on with his life. It was tremendously difficult for him, and on top of it all, a close family member had died during this same period.

After talking with him at length, I shared that I was writing a book and that I was trying to make some distinctions between hamster-wheel and potter's-wheel suffering. "What do you think?" I asked him. "Is there something that you would point to that would distinguish the two?

"Yes," he said. "Despite all of this pain and difficulty, the betrayal and the shame, there are moments of joy that keep invading my life. Jesus is with me in this, and that is sustaining me. To have joy spurt up in the midst of all this is ridiculous. And yet I keep being refreshed. I know I am not alone."

It is hard to work your way toward emotional freedom, just as it is hard for any slave to leave bondage. It was difficult for the southern slaves to work their way north toward freedom. It was hard for the Israelites to escape from Egypt, and it took courage to cross the Red Sea. It was difficult for Jews to escape Nazi Germany and flee concentration camps—many didn't.

When we read or watch accounts of terrible conditions of bondage and torture for so many people, all we want for them is freedom.

In the movie *The Shawshank Redemption*, Andy, the main character, is imprisoned for murdering his wife—a crime he didn't commit. The warden of the prison is corrupt, and he kills the one witness who could set Andy free. So over the years Andy slowly chisels a tunnel through his cell wall, hidden by a large poster of Rita Hayworth that hangs on his wall. One night Andy crawls through the tunnel he has made, swims through a putrid sewer and ends up outside the maximum security prison that has held him captive for so many years. "He's free!" you want to yell. "Yes! He made it! Run, Andy, run!" Andy does make it to freedom and begins a new life, but not until he brings about the downfall of the evil warden. The delight you feel for Andy is exhilarating.

I think that when we do an about-face on the things that keep us in bondage, God experiences that same delight. As Jesus tells us, "There will be more joy in heaven over one sinner who repents than over ninety-nine righteous persons who need no repentance" (Luke 15:7).

Sin means "missing the mark," as when an arrow shot from a bow goes wide of the target. We miss the mark when we live shackled to the hamster wheel. We miss the mark when we make someone other than God our god. We miss the mark when we decide there is no way of escape. But when we are liberated to stop going nowhere and to start going somewhere, the angels rejoice. "Yes!" they cry. "You've made it out. You've discovered the glorious liberty of the children of God!" The heavenly host throw a party. A banquet is held in your honor. That's more than a Shawshank redemption, that's an eternal redemption.

I see a lot of Christians walking around trying hard to be good people, and yet they're caught in a destructive cycle. Their behavior weighs them down as they slog on to "do God's will," having no idea that God's will is precisely *not* what they're doing. What glory does it give God for the world to see a bunch of morbid people dragging their baggage around, acting as if the resurrection never happened? No wonder unbelievers get turned off. All they have to do is look at God's people slumped over, worn out, dejected and depressed.

I am reminded of Kierkegaard's parable of the duck pastor who preached every Sunday to all the town's ducks at the church in the square. One day the duck pastor discovered that all ducks had wings and possessed the ability to fly! He couldn't wait until Sunday morning for his "flock" to arrive at church. "You know," he told them, "We can fly! We can soar! We are not land-bound. We can circle the skies!" The ducks in the congregation were impressed. "Great sermon!" they told the duck pastor. And then they all walked home.

Even if we believe the gospel, we can forget over time how wonderful the good news is. I remember starting a class I was teaching with a summation of the gospel message. I said, "Jesus died so that you could have a close, intimate relationship with God and live the abundant life right here on earth and forever in heaven with him. You are forgiven and you don't have to fear death anymore."

Someone yawned. Someone else looked forlornly at the snack table where the last piece of cake had just been taken. Others picked at their nails. This was a class of saints whom I regularly teach—some of the most active, stalwart members of our church.

"So," I said. "Why aren't you more excited?"

There was a moment's pause. Then they chuckled, then they laughed and finally they started clapping. They had heard it so many times they were used to it. Those of us who have been in church all our lives can suffer from long-term believers' glaze— a kind of spiritual hypnosis that hits us whenever we hear the standard gospel message, John 3:16, or other familiar truths. The truth doesn't penetrate the right way anymore. The way this class eventually applauded God was great. It was like they suddenly got it again, for the first time, and realized they could actually celebrate.

The gospel ought to pull the rug of normalcy out from under us and invite us into a life of daring love, lived-in hope and outrageous trust and celebration. We can't live in the hamster wheel with those attitudes. If we lived what we said we believed, we would leave church excited, encouraged and challenged to be daring and strong. Our statement of faith would be, "I believe in radical transformation through the grace and mercy of our Lord Jesus Christ. I will stake my life on it, live it, act it and do everything I can to grow. If God is for me, who can be against me? I entrust myself completely to the God who died for me. I will pursue healing, freedom and service in the name of Jesus Christ."

"But I don't know what God's will is for me," a young woman sobbed to me after I suggested the above. "It's all very nice what you say," she continued, dabbing tears with a tissue. "But I pray and I pray and I just don't know what to do."

Every so often God gives us CliffsNotes in Scripture—little summations so that if we haven't gotten the truth by doing the "Bible in One Year" regimen, we can still get it. Jesus' "Bible for Dummies" was, "Look, the whole law and the prophets is summed up in the following—Love the Lord your God with all your heart, soul and mind and your neighbor as yourself" (Luke 10:27). A quick and dirty version for the confused, time-constrained dropout. God also sums it up for us in Micah 6:8: "And what does the LORD require of you but to do justice, and to love kindness, and to walk humbly with your God?"

If you have read this whole book and still don't know "what to do," take these summations of Scripture to heart. Knowing that you cannot please everyone and that you were made to please God, ask yourself, "What does the Lord require of me?"

To do justice. Justice is more than fairness. Fairness tries to make external circumstances equal, but justice isn't based on external appearance. Justice values people, circumstances, motivation and context. It takes into account the entire picture. God is a God of justice, and you cannot further justice for others if you haven't pursued it for yourself. To stay put and refuse to name the problem does not perpetuate justice; it creates a downward spiral into hamster-wheel frenzy. God doesn't value the external; God looks beyond and sees the whole picture completely. Are you in need of God's justice for yourself or another? Pursue it!

To love mercy. Mercy wants to create a world full of merciful people, not perpetuate violence and oppression. Mercy is not feeling sorry for people; it is doing what will most help them to be whole. Sometimes this is tricky as we navigate the complexity of enabling versus helping. Are we keeping an unmerciful situation going by giving in and not rocking the boat? Or are we assisting in someone's ultimate recovery? We can ask this of our own situation as well. Is our lack of initiative in getting out of the hamster wheel actually intensifying unmerciful conditions? Do you need mercy today? Act on it.

To walk humbly with your God. Humility is only true humility when it comes out of a sense of our own worth in God's eyes. Passivity is not humility. Fear is not humility. Groveling is not humility. Humility comes out of a deep knowledge that we are loved and held secure. We don't have to prove anything anymore. We have One on our side who is utterly reliable, utterly faithful, utterly for us. This gives us courage to move forward and walk with God in dependence and trust, to move to the rhythms of justice, love and mercy that set us free. Live in the joyful reality of this empowering dependence.

Epilogue

It took me a while to decide to share my story. I hesitated because I was worried about what people would think of me. Then one day I decided I didn't care. I realized that if I shirked from telling it, I was negating the power of God that had kept me sane and alive during years of insanity. At first I shared with trembling, but gradually it became easier. I am convinced that it is the most helpful thing I have to offer people, and in a very real sense it is all I have to offer. What is more convincing to people of Christ's love and power than our own stories of his faithfulness? How do we prove the resurrection to Thomas? By showing our wounds (John 20:26-28).

People ask me about my mother, and I have to tell them that I really don't know much about her anymore. She is still alive, but for the safety of my children and my own stability, I have made the choice not to have contact with her. I have been honest and told her she needs help, but I don't think she will ever accept this. Do I pray for her? Yes. Have I forgiven her? Absolutely—although it took a while. One day I came upon a definition of resentment that startled me. Resentment, according to this definition, was feeling the same thing over and over. In my case, a negative, hardened and judgmental attitude toward my mother kept cycling through my life, like circling planes with nowhere to land. These circling planes of negative emotion were draining my energy and focus. Gradually I have let those planes come down through forgiveness.

The harder person to forgive was my father, but I have worked my way through that one as well. He was intelligent, creative and entertaining—trained at Menninger, a bastion of charm, genius and wit. I don't know why he couldn't seem to get my mother the help she needed, but for whatever reason it was beyond him. He helped many people to know Jesus, and what he provided in love gave me just enough fiber to survive. He wasn't always there, but he was there enough.

Anne Lamott has said in *Bird by Bird* that resentment is like drinking rat poison and waiting for the rat to die. That is not how I want to spend the rest of my days. I want to live, really live, in joy and not let life pass me by. As my therapy continues to unfold, as my prayer life deepens, as my trust in God increases, I find myself noticing things I have never noticed before. I am more amazed and full of wonder at the richness of life each year, like a kid gawking at a banana split for the first time—the ripples of whipped topping, the different colors of ice cream, the swirling fudge sliding off the side.

Yes, the rich texture of life amazes me. I look at my children and can scarcely believe the miracle that they are, growing up beautiful, healthy, competent and—inevitably—much taller than me. I love to ocean kayak with them and Tim, and I marvel at the expansive Pacific. I appreciate it like a gift—the gulls calling, the loons dipping and the sea lion popping above the surface of the water to stare at me with bright black eyes. It is as if I am finally alive, feeling, breathing, taking in grace.

One day I went to look at the yard I used to play in as a child. Of course it had shrunk beyond belief. The tree I had climbed was much shorter, and a branch I used to sit on had been sawed off. The wooden fence was still there, dark and moist from a recent rain, and on one end webs of leafless ivy sprawled up the side. Dirty snow and mud surrounded the bottom of the fence posts. I remembered how daunting that fence had seemed to me—high and severe with no places to peek through. Now I could easily look over the top and see a child playing basketball in the neighbor's driveway and the newly remodeled playground across the street. The yard was flat where I had played out so much of my young life. That small square of patchy lawn and stained snow had been my entire world for a long time.

I think about Jesus. He came from a wide expansive place to our meager plot of stained soil called Earth. When he came he pointed beyond our fences, beyond the flatness of life. He tried to show us that if we would just have the courage to listen and trust, life expands in all glorious directions. If we allowed him, he would lift us up and over to experience the glorious liberty of the children of God.

We hold in tension the reality of our current condition and the already/not-yet promise that "death will be no more; mourning and crying and pain will be no more" (Revelation 21:4). We catch glimpses of the fulfillment of this promise now during our earthly journey—healings, conversions, new inspirations, being aware of God's presence. We see in a glass dimly, but one day we shall see face to face.